A quilting bee in full buzz: Original drawing by L.L. Broadfoot from his book *Pioneers of the Ozarks*, copyright 1944. Reproduced by permission of Caxton Press, Caldwell, Idaho.

STAR QUILTS II

More of the Legendary
Kansas City Star Quilt Patterns

By the staff of The Kansas City Star

Kansas City Star Books
Kansas City, Missouri

STAR QUILTS II

Consultant and Contributor
Edie McGinnis

Editors
Monroe Dodd
Joyce Shirk

Illustrations, design and production
Jean Donaldson Dodd

Photography
Tammy Ljungblad

Illustrations:
Cover: Photo by Tammy Ljungblad
Page i: The Dragon Fly
Facing page, from left: Anna's Choice, Double Arrow, Arkansas Cross Roads
Back cover, from left: Top row: The Dragon Fly, Memory Bouquet, sampler quilt of patterns in *Star Quilts;* bottom row: The Sail Boat, Thrifty, Winding Blades.

Published by KANSAS CITY STAR BOOKS
1729 Grand Blvd.
Kansas City, Missouri, USA 64108

First edition

Library of Congress Card Number: 00-106617

ISBN 0-9679519-3-3

Printed in the United States of America by Walsworth Publishing Co.

To order copies, call StarInfo, (816) 234-4636.

www.kcstar.com

www.pickledish.com

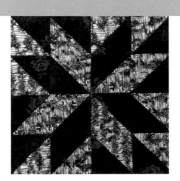

TABLE OF CONTENTS

Star-pattern quilt inspired by *Star Quilts*, published in 1999. Quilt made by Betty Haynie of Gladstone, Mo.

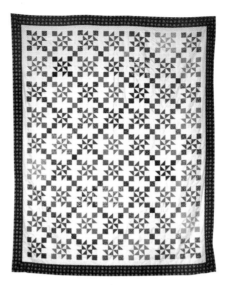

The Flying X, a 1938 pattern.

INTRODUCTION

A newspaper is one of life's timeliest commodities and, of course, also one of its most perishable. A newspaper replaces itself every day. Every day, it produces a new batch of articles and illustrations about our changing world, aiming always to avoid repeating "yesterday's news."

That's one reason that we at *The Kansas City Star* are so proud of the traditional quilt patterns we published from the late 1920s into the 1960s. Those patterns never became yesterday's news. They have lived on in innumerable quilts and in scores of private collections of newspaper clippings.

The *Kansas City Star* building, 18th Street and Grand Avenue, 1920s.

Today, Kansas City Stars are world famous. They've been indexed and reprinted over the years in various forms by various groups. In 1999, *The Kansas City Star* itself decided to publish its own book on these renowned patterns. *Star Quilts* told the history of the patterns, presented redrafts so modern-day quilters could make their own Stars and more. It was an immediate hit.

Yet there were too many Stars — more than 1,000 were printed in the newspaper through the years — and too much history for a single book.

That's why we're pleased to present *Star Quilts II.*

In these pages you'll find brand-new redrafts and cutting instructions, all easy to understand and colorfully illustrated, for 16 quilts that weren't in the first book.

Then you'll find the original patterns for the Memory Bouquet applique quilt, 20 of them, originally printed in *The Star* in autumn 1930.

We'll also bring you 12 quilting designs for empty squares.

And we'll show you some new ideas for combining and arranging your Star blocks, a great way to jump-start your own creativity.

As with the first *Star Quilts*, we've included a list of every pattern ever published in *The Kansas City Star*, by month and year.

Good luck and happy quilting!

CONTRIBUTORS

The organization of *Star Quilts II* is the brainchild of **Edie McGinnis**, a devotee of The Stars who also happens to be an employee of *The Kansas City Star.* She selected the patterns, prepared the redrafts, wrote the directions and made each one. She also chose the Memory Bouquet applique quilt and the quilting patterns.

Jean Dodd of *The Star,* besides designing the book and preparing the diagrams, came up with new ideas for combining and arranging Star blocks.

Nell Snead

The original contributors, of course, were the three artists who drew the patterns for the newspaper. They worked under the watchful eye of **Nell Snead**, who was woman's editor and fashion editor of *The Star* from the 1920s to the early 1960s. Snead sought patterns from quilters in the region and these artists prepared them for the newspaper.

Edie McGinnis.

Ruby Short McKim, circa 1928

■ **Ruby Short McKim** was the original Star quilt artist.

An Independence, Mo., businesswoman, she worked as the art needlework editor for *Better Homes & Gardens* magazine before founding McKim Studios in her hometown. McKim Studios grew into a national mail-order business for sewing patterns, kits and materials.

McKim drew Star patterns for the first three years.

Eveline Foland

■ **Eveline Foland** sketched the patterns over the next several years. She was a graphic designer who taught drawing at Manual Training High School, a vocational school in Kansas City.

Her patterns are known for their art-deco style and her distinctive signature.

One day Foland disappeared. Her last pattern was published unfinished and the following week an apology ran because pieces were missing. Many quilters now think Foland may have married and moved away or perhaps left *The Star* over a disagreement.

■ **Edna Marie Dunn** took over the patterns when Foland left.

Edna Marie Dunn at her drawing board at *The Kansas City Star* in the 1940s.

Dunn was *The Star's* fashion illustrator during her long tenure at the paper, 1914 to 1965. She also owned the Edna Marie Dunn School of Fashion in Kansas City.

Dunn's forte was selecting the most timeless designs from hundreds of quilt patterns readers submitted.

PATTERNS
AND REDRAFTS

In this first section you'll find 16 *Kansas City Star* quilts and instructions for making each of them. The description of each quilt begins with a reproduction of the original illustration as it was printed in *The Kansas City Star*. This illustration is accompanied by its original caption, although the type is reset because of the difficulty of reproducing consistently readable print from old newspapers. The captions retain the grammatical style of the original. For example, although *The Star* today abbreviates the word Kansas with "Kan." and the Post Office uses "KS," the newspaper in the old days used "Kas."

Next come modern instructions, complete with diagrams of the results you should expect. There's also a contemporary photo of each block as it should look when made. Occasionally, templates are shown with the instructions for use in cutting certain pieces. In most cases, the 16 patterns are accompanied by photos of entire quilts, some as many as 70 years old.

Stepping Stones (1931 pattern) **Made from family dress scraps by Mary R. Sorrels of Kansas City, Kan.**

STEPPING STONES MAY BE USED FOR A SIMPLE OR ELABORATE QUILT

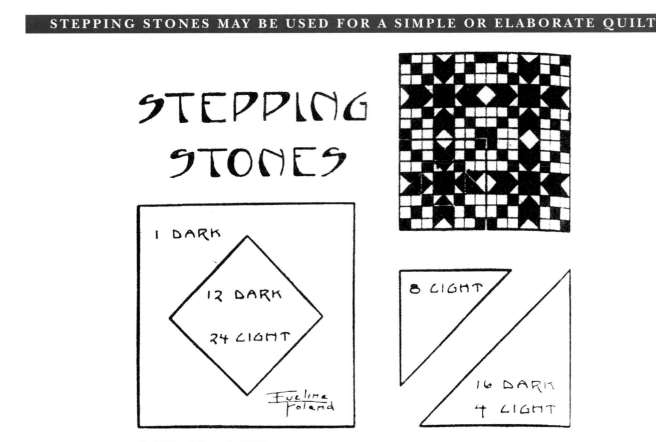

Published Sept. 9, 1931

The original instructions: **This pattern, "Stepping Stones," may be used in two ways. Either by setting the pieced blocks with a plain block or making the quilt of colored blocks which is an elaborate quilt. The cut shows the blocks and the lower left hand** [Editor's Note: These 1931 instructions should have said upper right hand] **corner shows how the blocks are combined. The pattern has pretty color combinations. This is a pretty pattern for a cushion.**

IN *THE STAR* THAT DAY...

E.W. Howe lived his life in country towns — mostly in Missouri and Kansas — yet became a nationally noted author, editor and philosopher. His first book, *The Story of a Country Town*, was rejected by every publisher to whom it was submitted. So in 1883 Howe printed it on the press of The *Atchison Globe*, the newspaper that he had founded six years earlier. He sent copies to Mark Twain and William Dean Howells. The two renowned authors praised Howe's work, and soon offers from publishing houses poured in.

In the history of American literature, *The Story of a Country Town* marked the beginning of a wave of realistic and unsentimental portrayals of rural life. In that book, in his newspaper and in brief columns like this one that appeared in the same issue of the weekly *Star* as the Stepping Stones pattern, Howe held a rather bleak view of human beings and their natures.

■ **Block size:** 12 inches
■ **Fabrics needed:** Three fabrics, a **light,** a **medium** and a **dark.**

CUTTING AND PIECING INSTRUCTIONS

NOTE: The following cutting measurements include a ¼-inch seam allowance.

■ From the **light** fabric, cut:
   * One 2-inch strip, 18 inches long.
   * One 3 ½-inch strip, 10 inches long.
   * Four 3 ½-inch by 2-inch rectangles.
   * Eight 2 ⅜-inch squares.

■ From **medium** fabric, cut:
   * One 2-inch strip, 18 inches long.
   * One 2-inch strip, 10 inches long.

■ From the **dark** fabric, cut:
   * One 3 ½-inch square.
   * Eight 2 ⅜-inch squares.
   * Four 3 ½-inch by 2-inch rectangles.

■ **Draw** a diagonal line from corner to corner on the back of the light 2 ⅜-inch squares. Place each light square atop a dark 2 ⅜-inch square, right sides facing.

■ **Sew** ¼ inch on both sides of the diagonal line. Cut along the line.

You will have 16 units like this:

■ **Sew** two half-square units together with light triangles touching, and two half-square units together with dark triangles touching. You will have units like these:

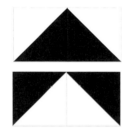

■ **Sew** each of these units to a dark rectangle, making a segment that looks something like the fletching on an arrow:

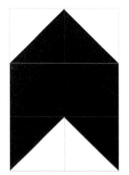

Using the remaining half-square units, make three more of these segments.

■ **Sew** the light 2-inch strip, 18 inches long, to the medium 2-inch strip, 18 inches long.

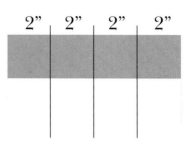

2" 2" 2" 2"

■ **Subcut** the strip into eight 2-inch segments. (You will have two inches extra length in case you need to straighten any cuts.) Sew these segments together to create a four-patch unit that looks like this:

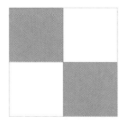

■ **Sew** a light 3 ½-inch rectangle to the side of the four-patch unit making sure the squares and rectangle match this diagram. Make four of these corner subunits.

■ **Sew** the medium 2-inch by 10-inch strip to the light 3 ½-inch strip. Subcut the strip into four 2-inch rectangles. (Again, you will have extra length for straightening purposes.)

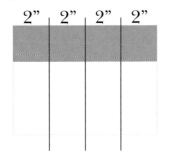

■ **Sew** these segments to the corner subunit making four corner units that look like this:

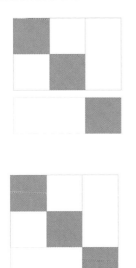

■ **Assemble** the block in three rows. The first row will consist of a corner unit, an arrow unit and another corner unit. The next row will be an arrow unit, the 3 ½-inch square and another arrow unit. The last row is the same as the first. Here's how it should look:

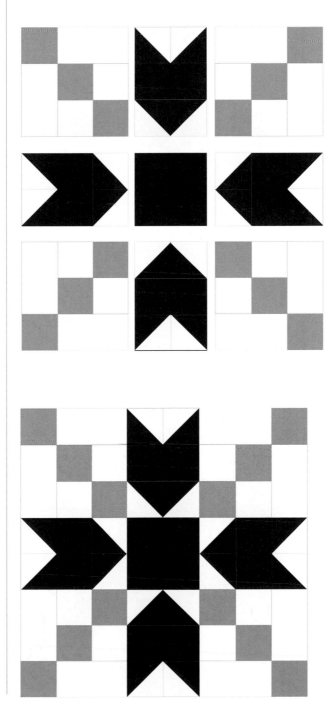

Stepping Stones block

Made by Edie McGinnis

Stepping Stones quilt (1931 pattern)   **Made by Virginia McGuire of Raytown, Mo.**

THE DOUBLE ARROW IS A CLEVER PATTERN

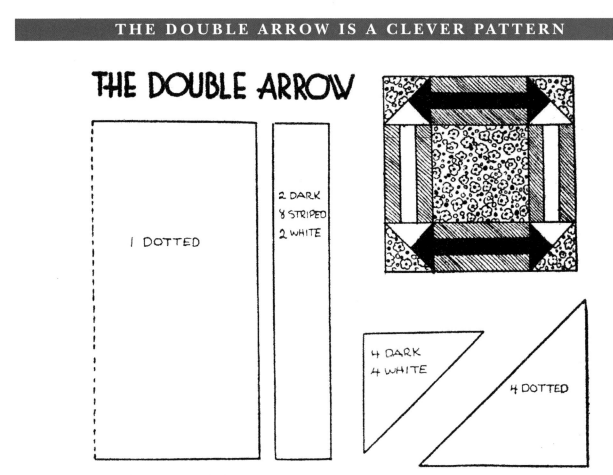

THE DOUBLE ARROW

1 DOTTED

2 DARK
8 STRIPED
2 WHITE

4 DARK
4 WHITE

4 DOTTED

Published June 24, 1933

The original instructions: **This is a pattern that invites the use of a dark and a light arrow. Some quiltmakers use a red and a green or a black and a white arrow. The latter combination is effective. Allow for seams. A quilt fan, Mrs. Minnie Townsend, Quenemo, Kas., sent the pattern to** *The Star.*

IN *THE STAR*...

Signs of the times in 1933 were these articles on the front page of the Saturday *Star*, the same day the Double Arrow pattern was printed inside. "McGee Tells More" recounted the police questioning of George McGee, who had confessed to the recent kidnapping of Mary McElroy, daughter of Kansas City's powerful city manager. The McElroy kidnapping, like those of drugstore magnate Michael Katz in 1930 and wealthy dress manufacturer Nell Donnelly in 1931, symbolized an era of high-profile crimes. Most infamous of those locally had occurred only a week before this newspaper was printed — the Union Station massacre.

On the economic front, "10,000 Road Jobs" heralded the delivery of $400 million in federal money for highway construction in Missouri. The money, officials hoped, would create 10,000 new jobs for a state weary of the Great Depression.

■ **Block size:** 12 inches
■ **Fabrics needed:** Four fabrics, a **light**, a **medium light**, a **medium** and a **dark**.

CUTTING AND PIECING INSTRUCTIONS

NOTE: The following cutting measurements include a ¼-inch seam allowance.

■ From the **light** fabric, cut:
  * One 4¼-inch square.
  * One 1½-inch strip, 14 inches long.

■ From the **medium light** fabric, cut:
  * Four 1½-inch strips, each 14 inches long.

■ From the **medium** fabric, cut:
  * Two 3⅞-inch squares.
  * One 6½-inch square.

■ From the **dark** fabric cut:
  * One 4¼-inch square.
  * One 1½-inch strip, 14 inches long.

■ **Draw** a diagonal line from corner to corner on the back of the light 4¼-inch square. Place the light square atop the dark 4¼-inch square, right sides facing.

■ **Sew** ¼ inch on both sides of the diagonal line. Cut along the line.

■ **Unfold** and press toward the dark fabric. You will have two units that look like this:

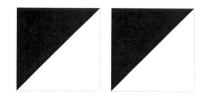

■ **Cut** these two units from corner to corner as shown. You will have four units that look like this. These are quarter-square triangles.

■ With your rotary cutter, **cut** the two medium 3⅞-inch squares from corner to corner. Sew a medium triangle to a quarter-square triangle, making units that look like this:

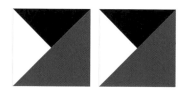

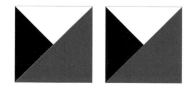

■ **Sew** two medium light strips to both sides of the light strip. Subcut the strip into two pieces 6½ inches long.

■ **Sew** these segments to each side of the 6½-inch medium square. (The extra inch called for in the cutting directions allows you to recut the edges if necessary to straighten them.)

■ **Sew** two medium light strips to both sides of the dark strip. Subcut the strip into two pieces, each 6 ½ inches long.

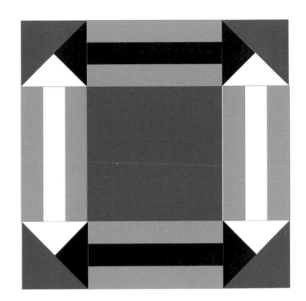

■ **Sew** a quarter-square triangle unit to each end of the strip, making sure the dark triangle touches the dark strip. You will then have units that look like this:

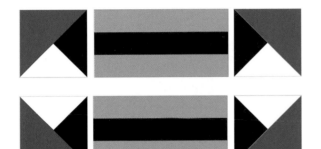

■ **Assemble** the units and the remaining pieces as shown.

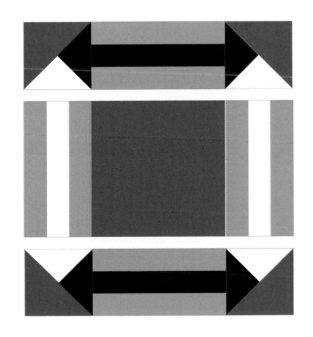

The Double Arrow block

Made by Edie McGinnis

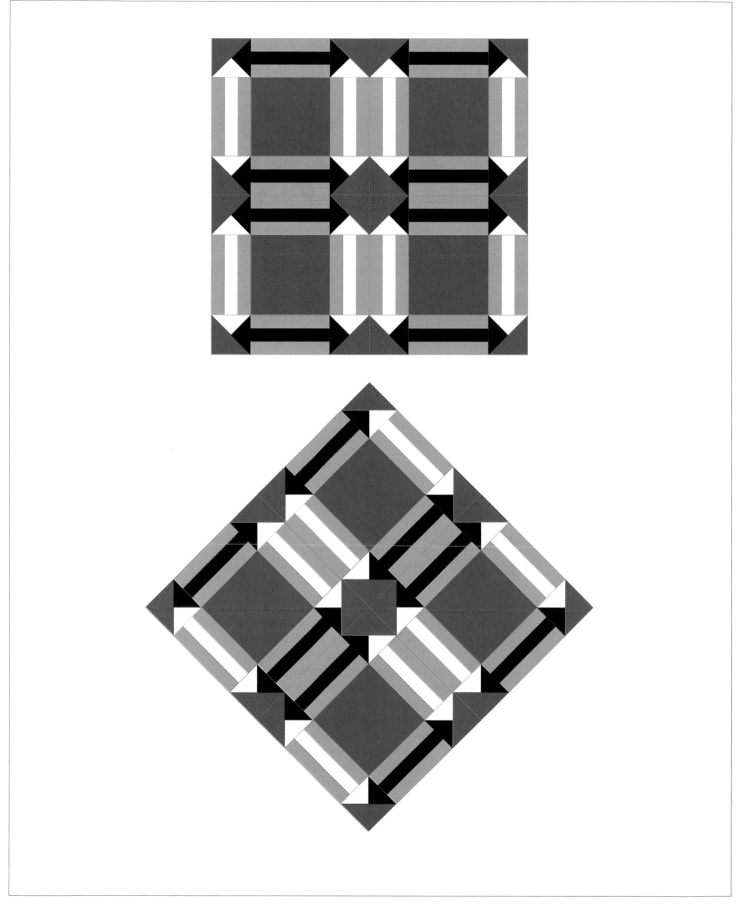

Crystal Star block

Made by Edie McGinnis

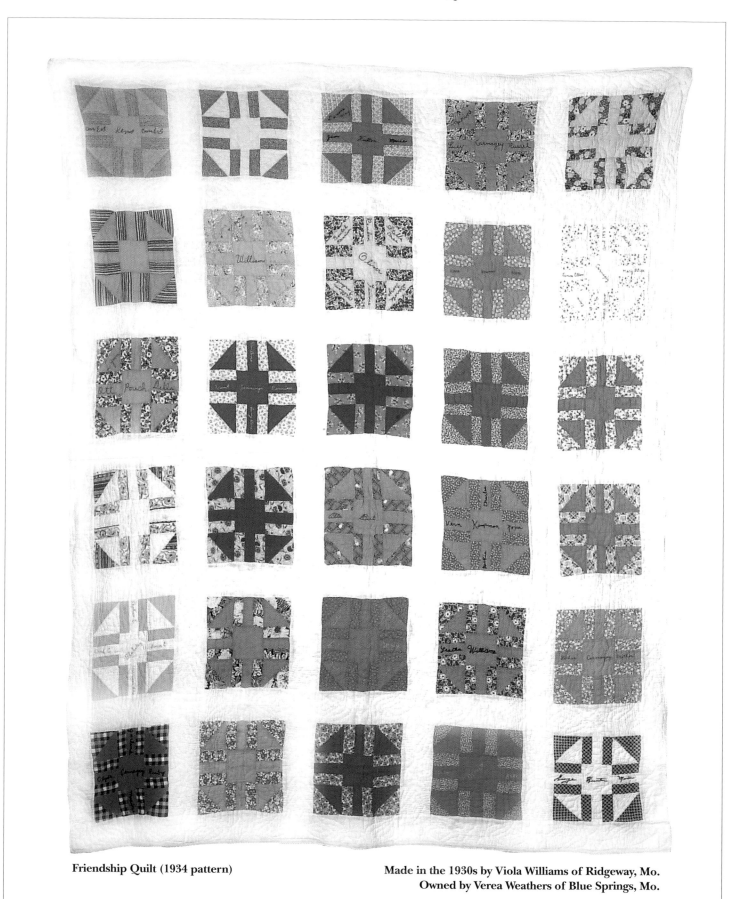

Friendship Quilt (1934 pattern)

**Made in the 1930s by Viola Williams of Ridgeway, Mo.
Owned by Verea Weathers of Blue Springs, Mo.**

ANOTHER VERSION OF THE FRIENDSHIP QUILT

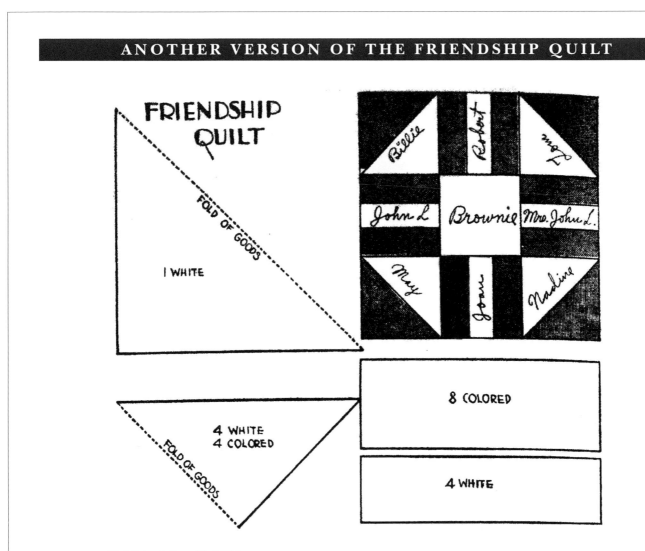

Published Oct. 31, 1934

The original instructions: **Here is another version of the Album quilt which is again popular as those made a generation ago. Allow for seams.**

IN *THE STAR*...

Life on the farm was tough in the 1930s. The worldwide depression had caused prices to plunge and meeting mortgage payments became hard for many farmers. The farm values described in this advertisement from *The Star*, published the same day as the Friendship Quilt pattern, show a 220-acre parcel with eight-room house and two barns going for less than $100,000 in Year 2000 money.

- **Block size:** 12 inches
- **Fabrics needed:** Three fabrics, a **light**, a **medium** and a **dark**.

CUTTING AND PIECING INSTRUCTIONS

NOTE: The following cutting measurements include a ¼-inch seam allowance.

- From the **light** fabric, cut:
  * One 1 ¾-inch strip, 19 inches long.
  * One 4 ½-inch square.
  * Two 4 ⅞-inch squares.

- From the **medium** fabric, cut:
  * Two 1 ⅞-inch strips, each 19 inches long.

- From the **dark** fabric, cut:
  * Two 4 ⅞-inch squares.

- On the two light 4 ⅞-inch squares, draw a diagonal line from corner to corner on the wrong side of the fabric. Place each of these light squares atop a dark 4 ⅞-inch square, right sides facing.

- **Sew** ¼ inch on both sides of the line. Cut along the line.

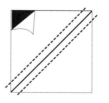

- **Unfold** and press toward the darker fabric.

You will have four units that look like this. These are the corner units.

- **Sew** a medium strip to each side of the light strip. Subcut the unit into 4 ½-inch pieces, making units that look like this:

4 ½"

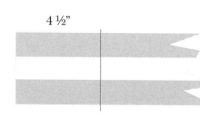

- **Sew** a corner unit to each end of one of the strip segments. Make two units like this:

- **Sew** a strip unit to two sides of the light square, making one unit that looks like this:

- **Assemble** the block as shown.

This block provides nine spaces for signatures.

Friendship Quilt block   **Made by Edie McGinnis**

A block from the Friendship Quilt, p. 18

Made in the 1930s by Viola Williams of Ridgeway, Mo.
Owned by Verea Weathers of Blue Springs, Mo.

Dragon Fly Quilt (1936 pattern)

Made by Ida Petersen of Royal, Iowa.
Owned by Gene South of Unity Village, Mo.

THE DRAGON FLY IS A LOVELY QUILT

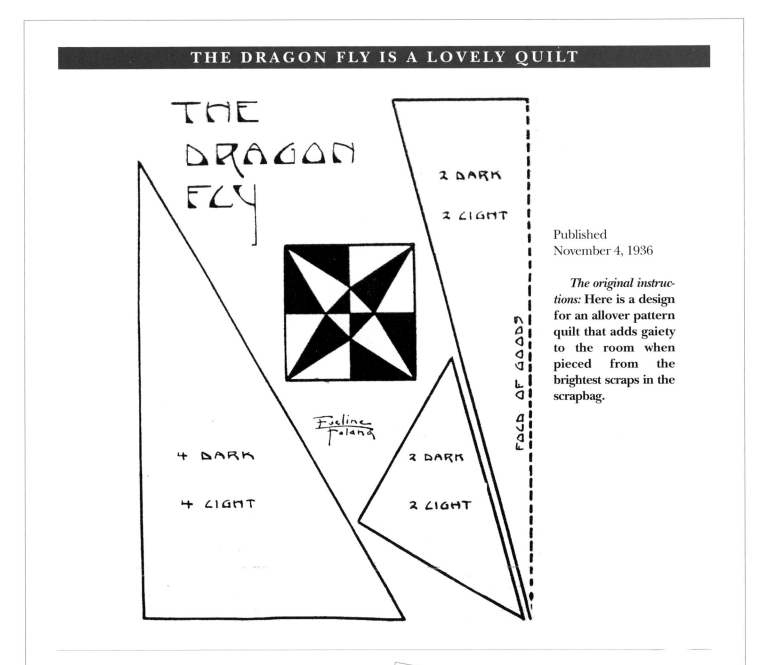

THE DRAGON FLY

Eveline Foland

2 DARK
2 LIGHT

4 DARK
4 LIGHT

2 DARK
2 LIGHT

FOLD OF GOODS

Published
November 4, 1936

The original instructions: **Here is a design for an allover pattern quilt that adds gaiety to the room when pieced from the brightest scraps in the scrapbag.**

IN *THE STAR*...

On Nov. 4, 1936, the weekly *Star* brought news of President Franklin D. Roosevelt's re-election by a landslide. Aided by western and southern farmers, industrial workers and a middle class that was starting to regain confidence during the Great Depression, Roosevelt carried 46 states. Among those was the home state of his Republican opponent, Alf Landon of Kansas.

Kansas City Star
LARGEST FARM WEEKLY
NESDAY, NOVEMBER 4, 1936.

AVALANCHE OF FAITH

Greatest Vote of Confidence Given Any President Is Recorded for Franklin Roosevelt in Huge Outpouring of Voters.

TAKES 46 STATES

Only in Maine and Vermont Does Alf M. Landon, the Republican, Gain a Majority.

POPULAR VOTE ROLLS HIGH

Margin of Victory, With 41 Million Ballots Cast, May Reach 9 Million.

■ **Block size:** 12 inches
■ **Fabrics needed:** Two fabrics, a **light** and a **dark**.

CUTTING AND PIECING INSTRUCTIONS

NOTE: The following cutting measurements include a ¼-inch seam allowance.

■ From **light** fabric, cut:
 * Two triangles using template A.
 * Two triangles using template B.
 * Two triangles using template C.
 * Two triangles using template C reversed. Turn over the template so it represents a mirror image of itself.

■ From the **dark** fabric, cut:
 * Two triangles using template A.
 * Two triangles using template B.
 * Two triangles using template C.
 * Two triangles using template C reversed. Turn over the template so it represents a mirror image of itself.

■ **Sew** one light triangle A to a dark triangle B. Sew a light triangle C to the unit, then add a light triangle C reversed. This makes one quarter of the block. Make two of these units.

■ **Sew** one dark triangle A to a light triangle B. Sew a dark triangle C to the unit, then add a dark triangle C reversed. Make two of these units.

■ **Assemble** block as shown.

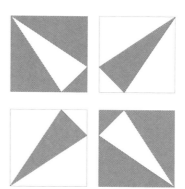

Templates
Use Templates A, B and C

Dragon Fly block

Made by Edie McGinnis

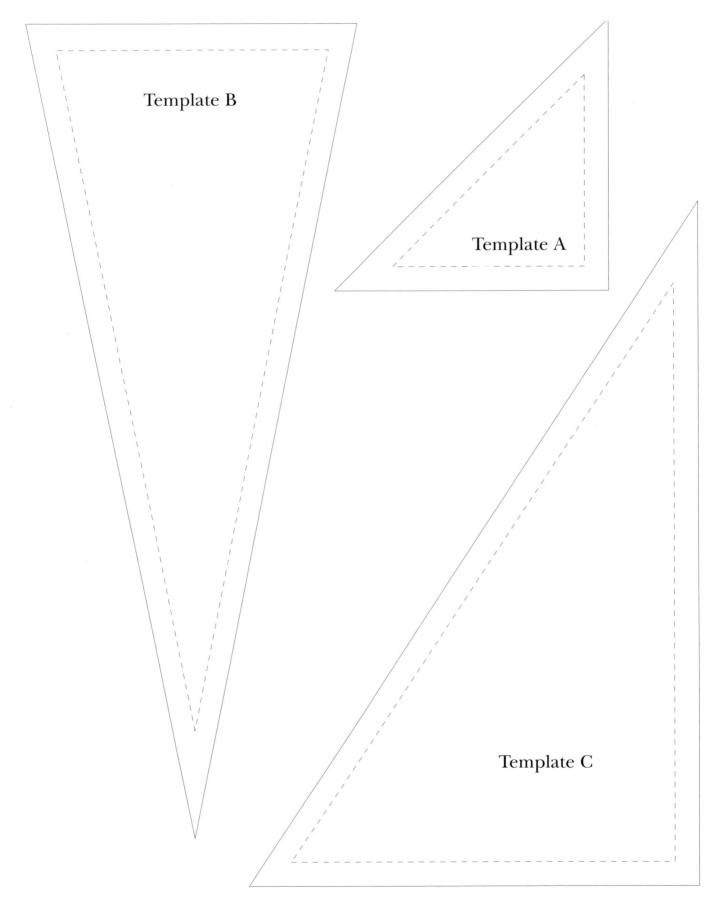

Template B

Template A

Template C

Indian Star block (1937 pattern) used as part of a quilt. See inset.   Made by Carol Weaver of Kansas City

STAR DESIGN IS ALWAYS POPULAR

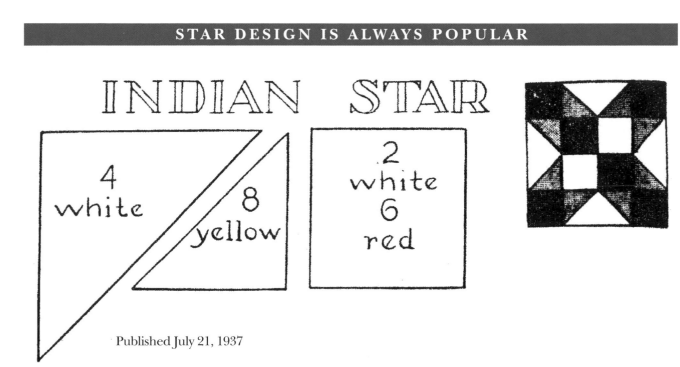

Published July 21, 1937

The original instructions: **Here is another version of the ever popular star design for a quilt. This pattern was contributed by Miss Genevieve Taylor, Bolivar, Mo.**

IN *THE STAR...*

Appealing to isolated rural families, RCA advertised its farm radio as providing "more distant stations ... greater volume ... finer tone." In addition, the ad pointed out that the radio could be run off "power from the air or gasoline power generator." Many parts of the country remained without electrical power service in 1937, so farmers had to find other sources. One was a generator powered by a windmill. These devices, called radio windmills, inspired a 1941 Star quilt pattern (See Page 61).

■ **Block size:** 12 inches
■ **Fabrics needed:** Three fabrics, a **light,** a **medium** and a **dark.**

CUTTING AND PIECING INSTRUCTIONS

NOTE: The following cutting measurements include a ¼-inch seam allowance.

■ From the **light** fabric, cut:
  * Two 3 ½-inch squares.
  * Four 3 ⅞-inch squares.

■ From the **medium** fabric, cut:
  * Four 3 ⅞-inch squares.

■ From the **dark** fabric, cut:
  * Six 3 ½-inch squares.

■ **Draw a diagonal line** from corner to corner on the wrong side of the light 3 ⅞-inch squares. Place each light 3 ⅞-inch square atop the medium 3 ⅞-inch squares, right sides facing.

■ **Sew** ¼-inch on both sides of the diagonal line. Cut on the line and press toward the medium fabric.

You will have eight units that look like this:

■ **Assemble** the units in rows as shown.

■ The finished block should look like this:

Indian Star block

Made by Edie McGinnis

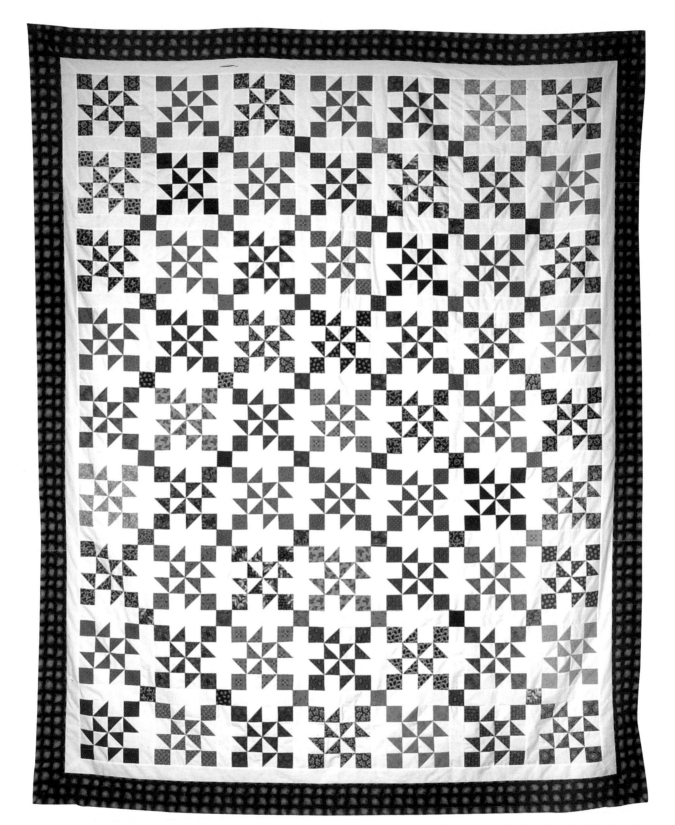

The Flying X quilt top (1938 pattern)   **Quilt top made by Cecilia Ash of Pekin, Ill.**

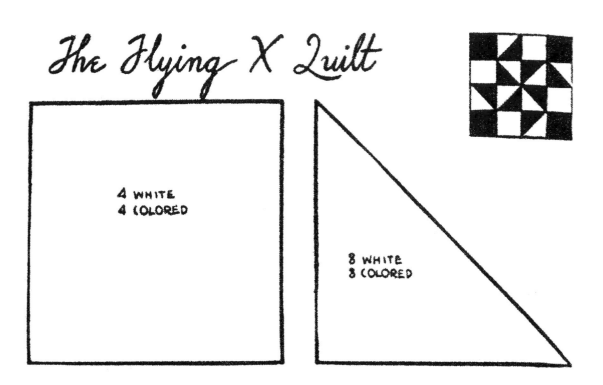

FLYING X IS AN EASY PATTERN

The Flying X Quilt

4 WHITE
4 COLORED

8 WHITE
8 COLORED

Published October 26, 1938

The original instructions: **The finished block of Flying X looks intricate, but the piecing of the block is simple. The pattern was contributed by Mrs. Lizzie Robinson, Anderson, Mo. Thank you.**

IN *THE STAR...*

Despite having made progress against the Great Depression, the country had problems throughout the 1930s. This advertisement, published the same day as Flying X, illustrates the continuing ill effects of the economy on farm life — liquidations.

■ **Block size:** 12 inches
■ **Fabrics needed:** Two fabrics, a **light** and a **dark**.

CUTTING AND PIECING INSTRUCTIONS

NOTE: The following cutting measurements include a ¼-inch seam allowance.

■ From the **light** fabric, cut:
  * Four 3 ½-inch squares.
  * Four 3 ⅞-inch squares.

■ From the **dark** fabric, cut:
  * Four 3 ½-squares.
  * Four 3 ⅞-inch squares.

■ **Draw** a diagonal line on the wrong side of each of the four light 3 ⅞-inch squares. Place each light 3 ⅞-inch square atop a dark 3 ⅞-inch square, right sides facing.

■ **Sew** ¼-inch on both sides of the diagonal line. Cut on the line.

■ **Unfold** each unit and press toward the dark fabric. You will have eight units that look like this:

■ **Assemble** the units in rows as shown.

■ The finished block should look like this:

Flying X block

Made by Edie McGinnis

Star and Box (1939 pattern)   **Made and owned by Peggy and Francis Hutinett of Raytown, Mo.**

THE STAR AND BOX QUILT

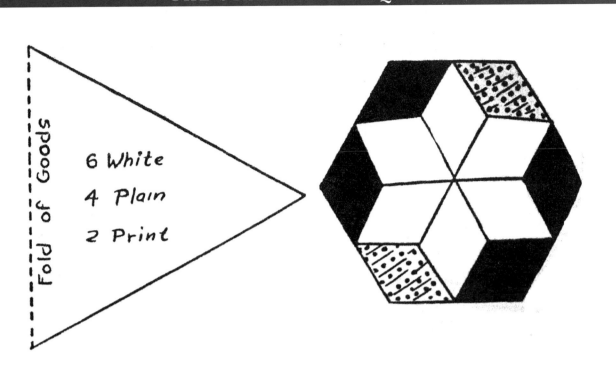

Fold of Goods

6 White
4 Plain
2 Print

Published Sept. 20, 1939

The original instructions: **Mrs. Karl Harms, Ionia, Mo., copied this pattern from a quilt that was made forty years ago. This all-over design is sometimes called Tumbling Blocks.**

IN *THE STAR*...

This pattern was published only 20 days after Adolf Hitler's German war machine pounded into Poland, beginning World War II. At the time, the capital of Warsaw was holding out against the advance but it would fall within a little more than a week. The headlines show the German dictator saying he wanted peace, but also warning Britain and France to drop their own declarations of war on Germany. Ominously, he said that Allied leaders "have been shown what the German Army can do."

GAUNTLET TO THE ALLIES

Germany Has No War Intention Against Either England or France, but Will Fight to a Finish if They Choose to Continue, Hitler Says.

LOOKS TO PEACE

Fuehrer Says Germany and Russia Will Solve Polish Situation and Remove Tension.

READY FOR A LONG WAR

Word Surrender Never Will Be Uttered, He Shouts in International Broadcast.

"Germans Once Oppressed by Treaty of Versailles May Live Again."

LAUDS MILITARY MIGHT

Allied Statesmen "Have Been Shown What the German Army Can Do."

A Map of the War Front.

An unusual map which shows the fortifications of the Maginot and Seigfried lines as they face each other on the border between France and Germany will be found on the editorial page. As it is along this western front that the big battles of the war now are expected to be waged, it is suggested that the map be clipped and saved.

END TO POLAND

Crushed Between German and Russian Armies, Nation Practically Ceases to Exist.

TO BE A 'PUPPET' STATE

Soviets and Germans to Take About Two-Thirds of the War-Torn Country.

With Present Government Fleeing, a New Polish Regime is Expected to Ask Peace.

WARSAW STILL HOLDS

Battered Capital Emerges From a Night of Shelling Still in Polish Hands.

■ **Fabrics needed:** Two fabrics, a **light** and a **dark**.

CUTTING AND PIECING INSTRUCTIONS

Because the Star and Box quilt is not made from square units, these instructions will show you how to make a corner of the quilt. You may use these instructions as the basis for a larger quilt.

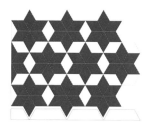

■ From **dark** fabric, cut:
  * 56 diamonds using Template A.
  * Two half-diamonds using Template A1.

■ From **light** fabric, cut:
  * 21 diamonds using Template A.
  * Two half-diamonds using Template A1.
    * Three pieces using Template B
    * One piece using Template B1.

■ For this quilt, it's important to mark the ¼-inch seam allowance on every piece of fabric.

Making a star:
■ **Place** two dark diamonds together, right sides facing. Stitch along marked seam line.

■ **Unfold** and press.

■ **Place** a third background diamond atop one of the original two, right sides facing. Stitch along marked seam line as shown.

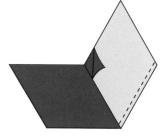

■ **Unfold** and press.

■ **Repeat** this process to make the other half of the star.

■ **Sew** the resulting two half-stars together, making sure the center points match. If you're sewing by machine, sew outward from the mid-dle of the block. Press each star.

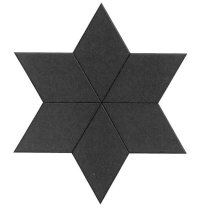

To make the quilt corner pictured, you'll need nine full stars and one half-star for the end of the middle row.

You'll make the quilt by assembling the stars in horizontal rows.

■ To one star, sew a diamond of light fabric by placing the diamond atop one edge of the star, right sides facing. Beginning at the inside point, stitch ¼-inch from the edge as shown. Make sure not to catch (sew over) any previously sewn seams.

■ Pivot the diamond and stitch along its other edge, as shown, again making sure not to catch previously sewn seams.

Templates

Use Templates A, A1, B and B1

■ **Use** this method every time you attach a diamond edge to a star edge. Sew the next star in the row to this diamond.

■ **Continue** this way on the row until three stars are assembled. You will need to make two of these rows. Attach a Template A1 piece to the left end of both rows.

■ Now **make** one more row, which will contain three full stars. Sew light diamonds on five sides of each star.

■ **Attach** the stars like this:

■ **Create** a half-unit like this using Template A and Template A1 pieces.

■ Attach this half-star to the left end of the row you have just made.

■ Assemble the three rows.

■ **Sew** the three Template B shapes to the bottom. In the corner, sew a Template B1 shape.

■ Using this pattern you can make a larger quilt.

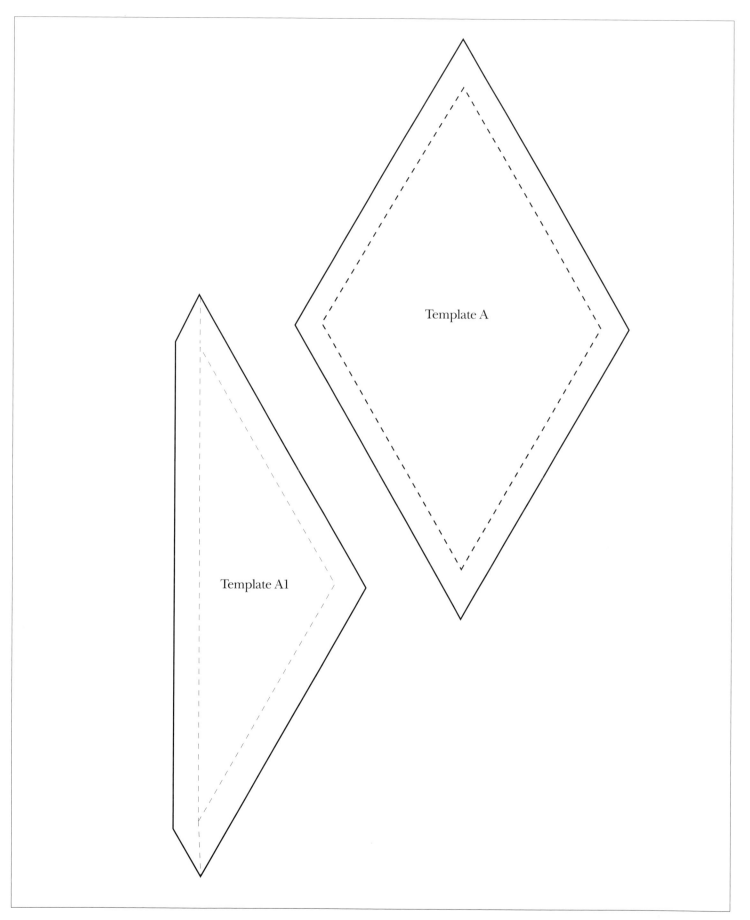

Template A

Template A1

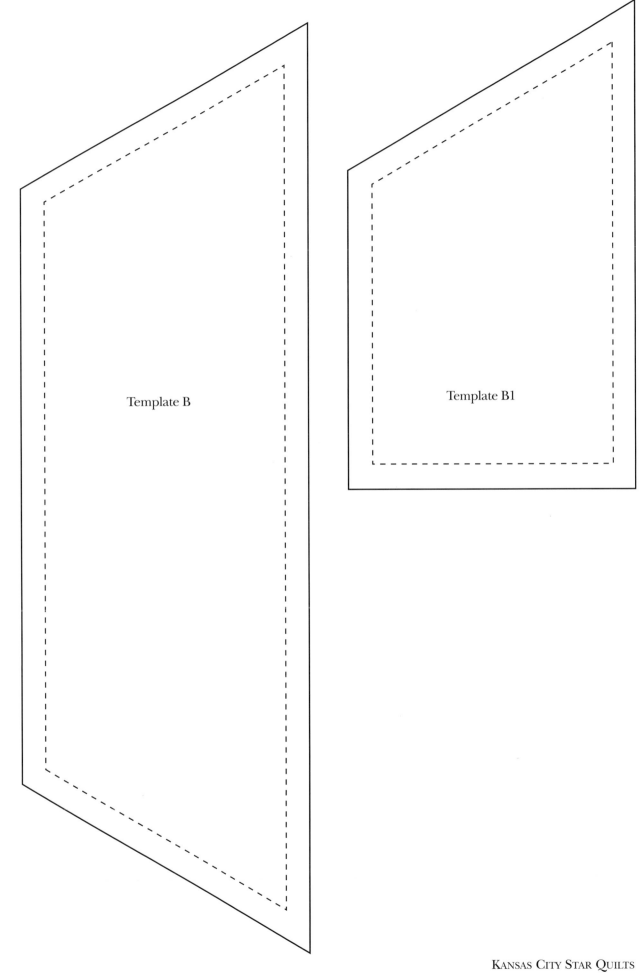

Template B

Template B1

Thrifty Quilt (1939 pattern)   **Courtesy of Smiths Antiques, Laclede, Mo.**

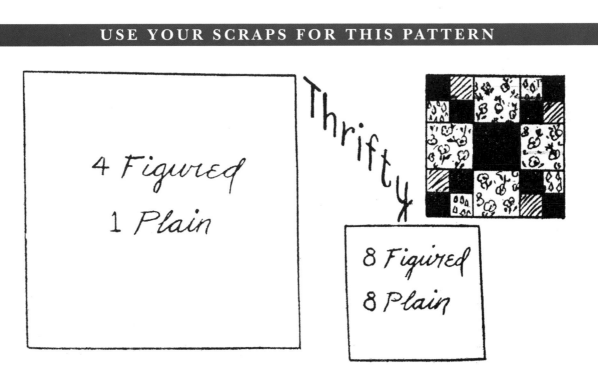

USE YOUR SCRAPS FOR THIS PATTERN

4 Figured
1 Plain

Thrifty

8 Figured
8 Plain

Published Dec. 27, 1939

The original instructions: **The idea for the Thrifty design originated by Mrs. Clarence Welker, Millersville, Mo. She chose this name for the pattern because she went to her scrap bag for the three kinds of print and the one-tone pieces required for it.**

IN THE STAR...

Despite the war raging in Europe, the weekly *Star's* wish for the upcoming year was for steady rains to wet the fields of mid-America.

The Weekl

(THE SOUT

KANS

OUR WISH FOR 1940.

Following the custom of wishing everyone a happy New Year, we believe this would be a good time to get practical and as long as we are wishing, make our wants concrete. Thus our wish for 1940 is that we have a year of normal rainfall, or even above normal. We hope that we get rain not only in the spring, but in the summer, fall and winter—that the crops not only may be promising in June but may reach maturity without being bleached and scorched. Since there is no reason for being conservative in a wish, may we add we would like to have the rains come as sod-soakers, not gully washers.

within a few weeks. They said that, inasmuch as domestic prices had **WALLACE FIRM ON PLAN**

■ **Block size:** 12 inches
■ **Fabrics needed:** Three fabrics, a **light,** a **medium** and a **dark.**

CUTTING AND PIECING INSTRUCTIONS

NOTE: The following cutting measurements include a ¼-inch seam allowance.

■ From **light** fabric, cut:
   * Four 4 ½-inch squares.
   * One 2 ½-inch strip, 11 inches long.

■ From **medium** fabric, cut:
   * One 2 ½-inch strip, 11 inches long.

■ From **dark** fabric, cut:
* One 4 ½-inch square.
* Two 2 ½-inch strips, each 11 inches long.

■ **Sew** a dark strip to the light strip. Press toward the dark fabric. Subcut the strip into four 2 ½-inch wide units. (The extra inch called for in the cutting directions allows you to recut the edges if necessary to straighten them.)

■ **Sew** the remaining dark strip to the medium strip. Press toward the dark fabric. Subcut the strip into four 2 ½-inch wide units.

2 ½"

■ **Join** the units as shown to make four 4-patch segments.

■ **Assemble** these segments with the remaining pieces as shown.

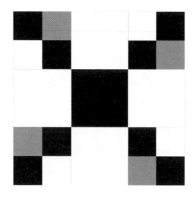

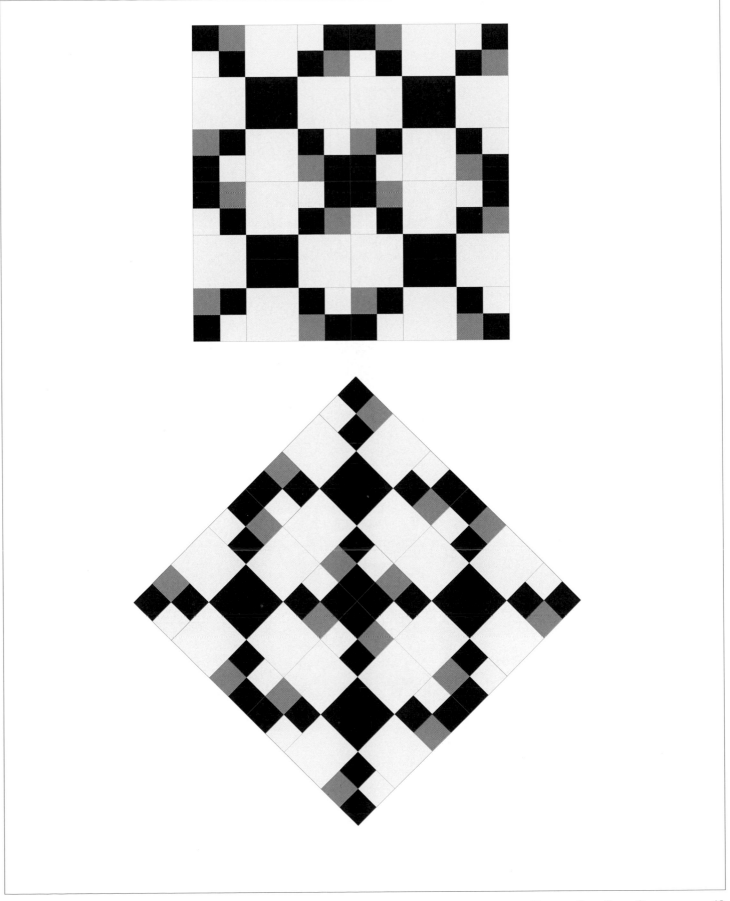

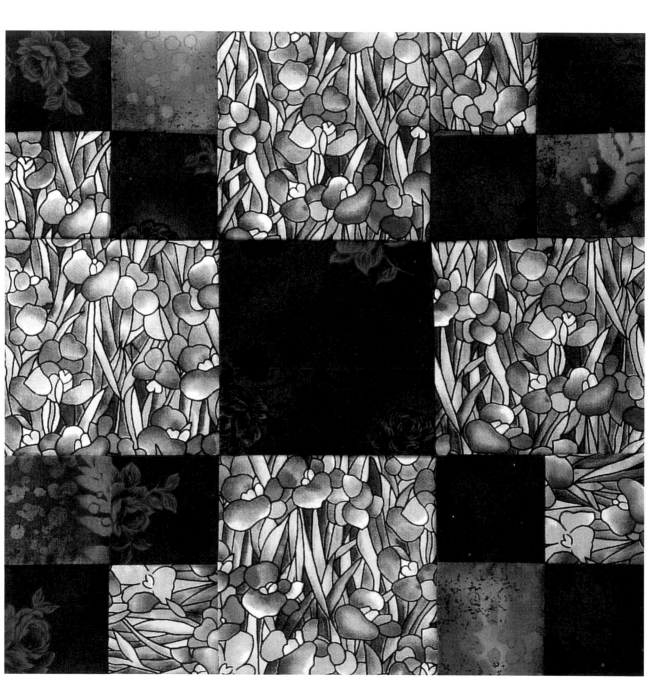

Thrifty block

Made by Edie McGinnis

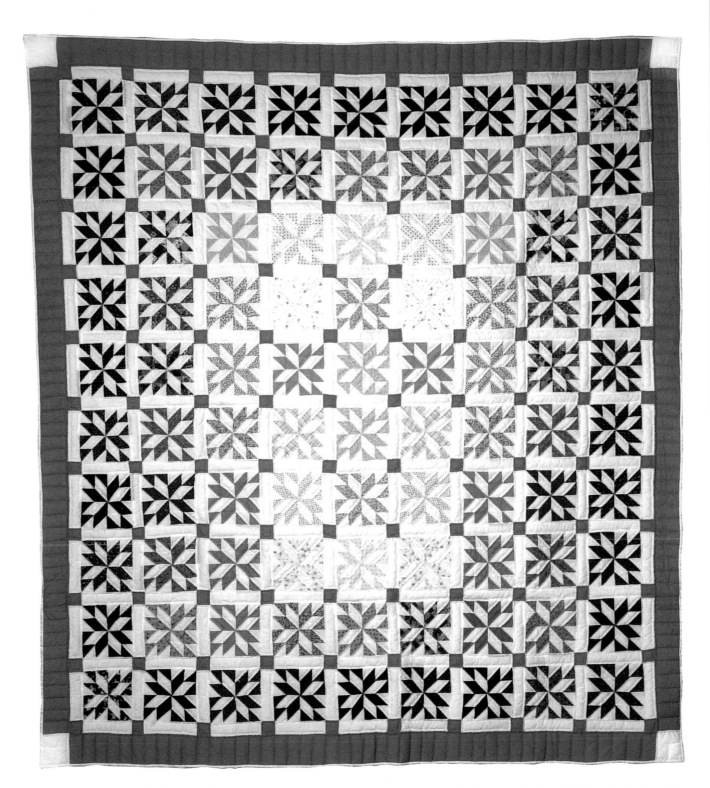

Anna's Choice quilt (1941 pattern)

**Made by Jan Neale of El Dorado Springs, Mo.
Owned by Anna Neale of Lebanon, Mo.**

ANNA'S CHOICE QUILT

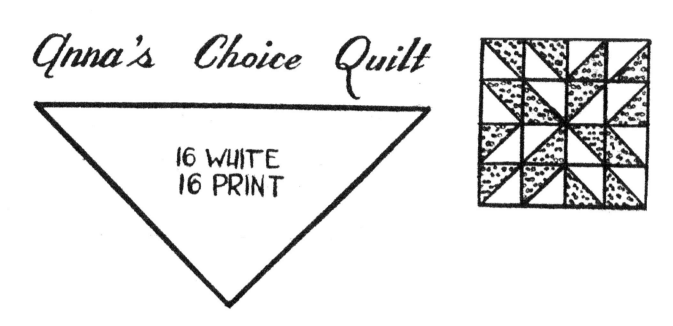

Published Feb. 26, 1941

The original instructions: **This very old pattern comes from Mrs. Dayton D. Noel, Unionville, Mo. She prefers the quilt developed in a combination of blue print and solid blue, using a 1-tone blue of the shade dominating in the print. Mrs. Noel started collecting quilt block patterns and designs for homemade articles reproduced in the *Weekly Star* in 1928 and now has 350 illustrations.**

IN *THE STAR*...

Wheat farmers of the Great Plains were staring at a problem in early 1941, when this pattern was published. They had produced big surpluses but the war in Europe destroyed that continent as a market for the excess. As part of the New Deal effort to help agriculture out of the depression, the government had involved itself in a big way with trying to prop up prices and buy excess commodities. Now, farmers were asking government what could be done. At the conference reported here by the weekly *Star*, the answer turned out to be: We don't know.

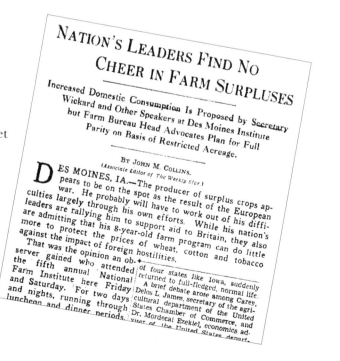

- **Block size:** 12"
- **Fabrics needed:** Two are used, one **dark** and one **light**.

CUTTING AND PIECING INSTRUCTIONS

NOTE: The following cutting measurements include a ¼-inch seam allowance.

- From **light** fabric cut:
  * Eight 3⅞-inch squares.
- From **dark** fabric cut:
  * Eight 3⅞-inch squares.

- **Draw** a diagonal line on the back of each dark square. Place each dark square on top of a light square, right sides facing.

- **Stitch** ¼ inch on either side of the diagonal line.

- **Cut** along the diagonal line and press the seam to the dark fabric. Repeat until you have 16 units like this:

- Assemble the units in rows, two rows like this:

- …and two rows that look like this:

- Assemble the rows into the full block, like this:

- The finished block should look like this:

Anna's Choice block　　　　　　　　　　　　　　　　**Made by Edie McGinnis**

Arkansas Cross Roads (1941 pattern)   **Quilt made by Peggy McFeeters of Morton, Ill.**

THE ARKANSAS CROSS ROADS

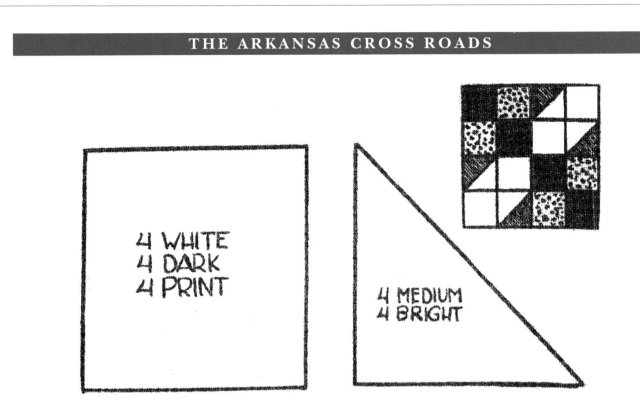

4 WHITE
4 DARK
4 PRINT

4 MEDIUM
4 BRIGHT

Published March 19, 1941

The original instructions: **This pattern which employs white pieces, print and 1-tone blocks in color is the creation of Mrs. Ed Martin, New Home farm, Gravette, Ark. She finds it is particularly adapted to the limited skill of beginners in needlework. Mrs. Martin is another subscriber who has long collected quilt designs from** *The Weekly Star.* **For the last ten years she has pasted them in a big book that she says "money couldn't buy."**

IN *THE STAR*...

Appealing to tenant farmers who might be worried that "someone else will come along and buy the farm you are living on," Opportunity Farms of Chillicothe, Mo., ran this advertisement the same day as the Arkansas Cross Roads pattern. "Today's prices," the company said, "are low and terms are easy."

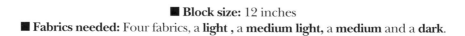

■ **Block size:** 12 inches
■ **Fabrics needed:** Four fabrics, a **light** , a **medium light**, a **medium** and a **dark**.

CUTTING AND PIECING INSTRUCTIONS

NOTE: The following cutting measurements include a ¼-inch seam allowance.

■ From the **light** fabric, cut:
  * Four 3 ½-inch squares.
  * Two 3 ⅞-inch squares.

■ From the **medium light** fabric, cut:
  * Four 3 ½-inch squares.

■ From the **medium** fabric, cut:
  * Two 3 ⅞-inch squares.

■ From the **dark** fabric, cut:
  * Four 3 ½-inch squares.

■ **Draw** a diagonal line from corner to corner on the wrong side of the two light 3 ⅞-inch squares. Place the two light squares atop the medium 3 ⅞-inch squares, right sides facing.

■ **Sew** ¼ inch on both sides of the diagonal line. Cut on the line and press toward the medium fabric.

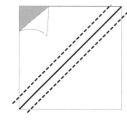

■ You will have four units that look like this:

■ **Assemble** the units in rows as shown.

■ The finished block should look like this:

Arkansas Cross Roads block

Made by Edie McGinnis

THE RADIO WINDMILL

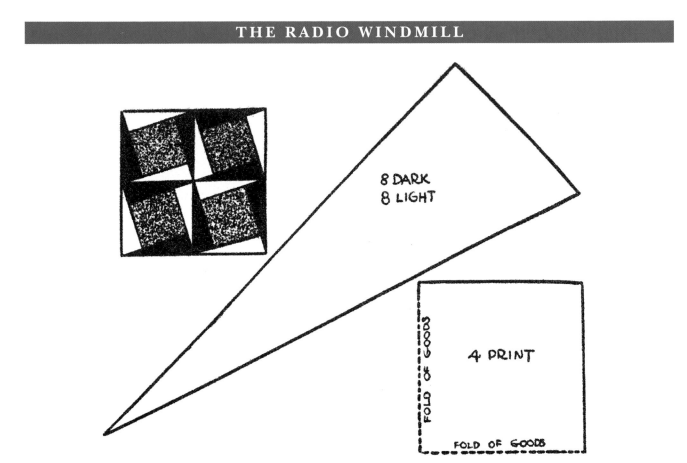

Published Oct. 22, 1941

The original instructions: **The contributor of this pattern, Miss Anna Killillay, Pleasanton, Ia., says it may be set with plain blocks or used as an allover pattern. If the latter plan is followed the quilt will show many small windmills all over the coverlet. For a combination she suggests a small print and two one-tone pieces.**

IN *THE STAR...*

Even though Pearl Harbor lay six weeks in the future, the country was busy making armaments for the Allies fighting Germany. This American Royal advertisement, published the same day as The Radio Windmill pattern, noted "Live Stock's Part in National Defense."

■ **Block size:** 12 inches
■ **Fabrics needed:** Three fabrics, a **light**, a **medium** and a **dark**.

CUTTING AND PIECING INSTRUCTIONS

NOTE: The following cutting measurements include a ¼-inch seam allowance.

■ From **medium** fabric, cut:
  * Four squares using Template B.

■ From **light** fabric, cut:
  * Eight triangles using template A. Align the fabric grain that parallels the selvage — called the straight of grain — with the arrow on the template.

■ From **dark** fabric, cut:
  * Eight triangles using template A. Align the straight of grain of the fabric with the arrow on the template.

■ NOTE: All fabric cut with template A must be cut with the right side of the fabric up. Do not fold to cut multiple pieces; this will create mirror-image pieces that will not fit this pattern.

■ **Sew** a light triangle partly to the bottom of a medium square, leaving the seam unsewn an inch or two as shown by the broken line in this diagram.

■ **Add** a dark triangle to the square.

■ **Add** another light triangle to the square.

■ **Add** another dark triangle to the square.

■ **Close** the seam left unsewn on the first triangle. This unit makes one quarter of the block. Make three more squares like this:

■ **Assemble** the block as shown. When used as an overall pattern, a secondary pattern of light and dark four-pointed stars emerges.

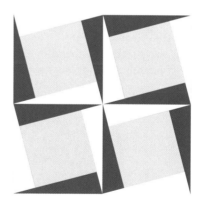

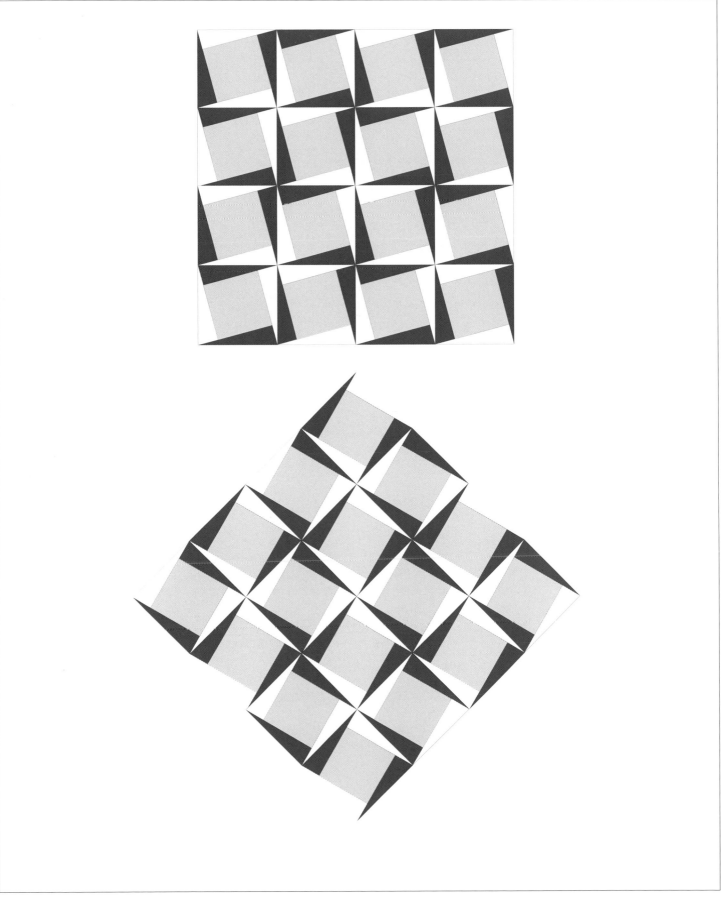

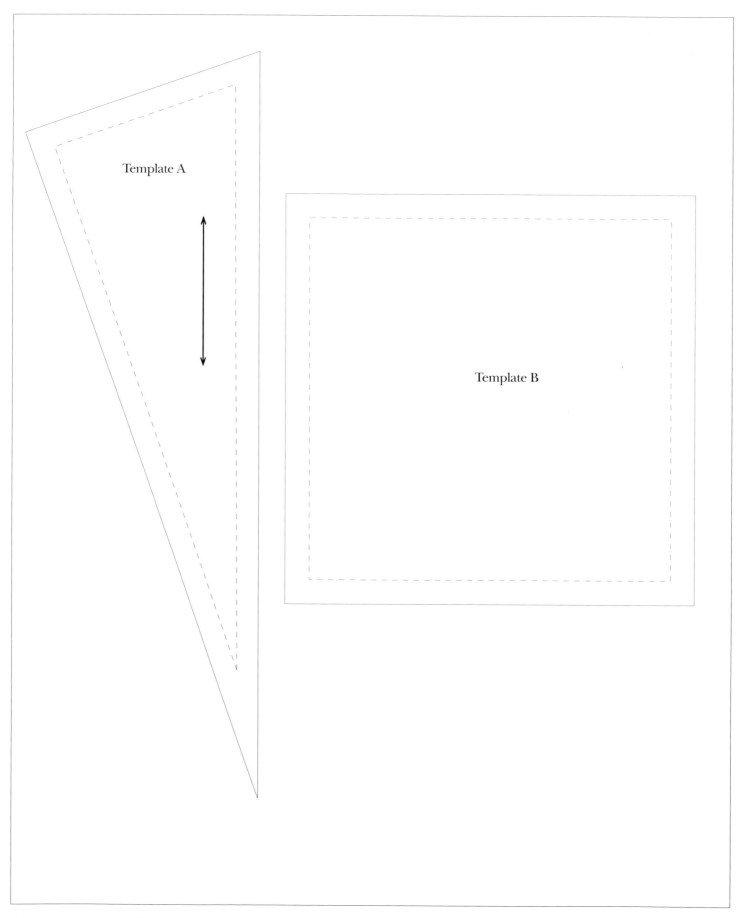

Template A

Template B

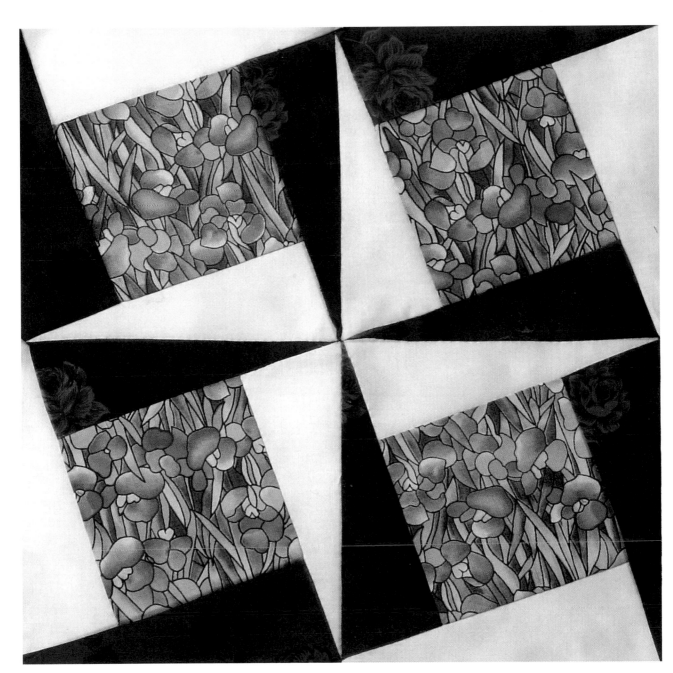

The Radio Windmill block

Made by Edie McGinnis

SIGNAL LIGHTS

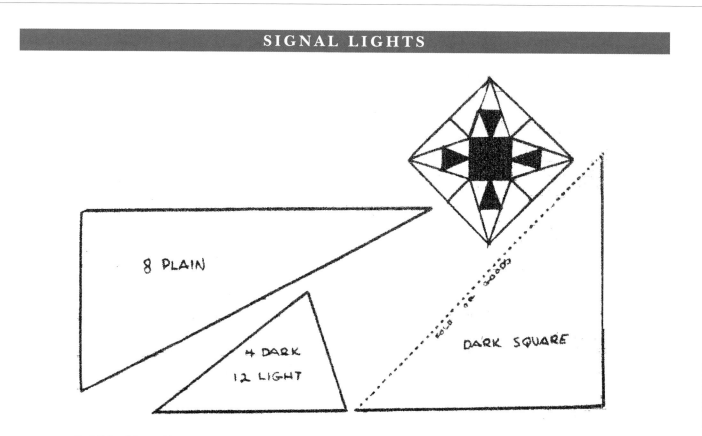

8 PLAIN

4 DARK

12 LIGHT

GOLD

DARK SQUARE

Published June 17, 1942

The original instructions: **Enthusiasm over quilt making spurred Mrs. B.R. Troutman, Ottumwa, Ia., to create designs of her own. This pattern is most effective in sharply contrasting light and dark blocks.**

IN *THE STAR*...

On the day Signal Lights was published by *The Star*, nationwide rationing was a proposal. It wouldn't take long to become reality. By the end of the war in 1945, the average driver was limited to purchasing two gallons of gasoline a week. Doctors, "essential workers" and others for whom driving was a necessity got to use more.

■ **Block size:** 12 inches
■ **Fabrics needed:** Three fabrics, a **light,** a **medium** and a **dark.**

CUTTING AND PIECING INSTRUCTIONS

NOTE: The following cutting measurements include a ¼-inch seam allowance.

■ From **light** fabric, cut:
  * Twelve triangles using Template C.

■ From **medium** fabric, cut:
  * One 4-inch square, using Template B.
  * Four triangles using Template C.

■ From **dark** fabric, cut:
  * Four triangles using Template A.

The points of the star are made up of four triangles, 3 light and one medium. Assemble like this:

■ **Make** four of these units and sew one to each side of the square.

■ **Add** the dark triangles to finish the block as shown.

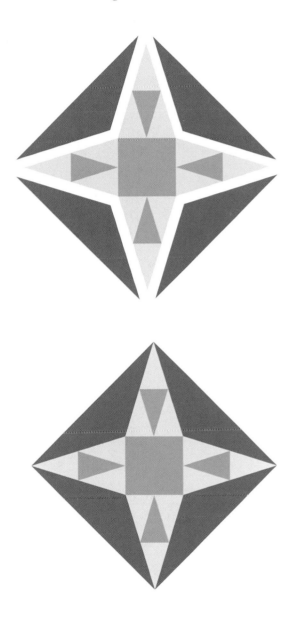

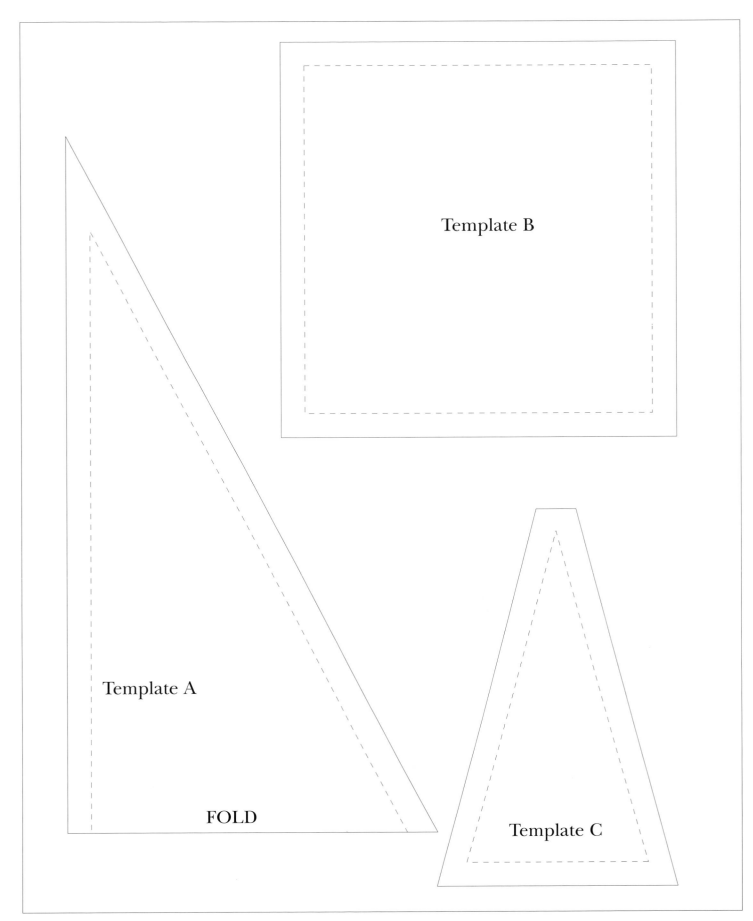

Template B

Template A

FOLD

Template C

Signal Lights block

Made by Edie McGinnis

Winding Blades quilt   **Courtesy of Smiths Antiques, Laclede, Mo.**

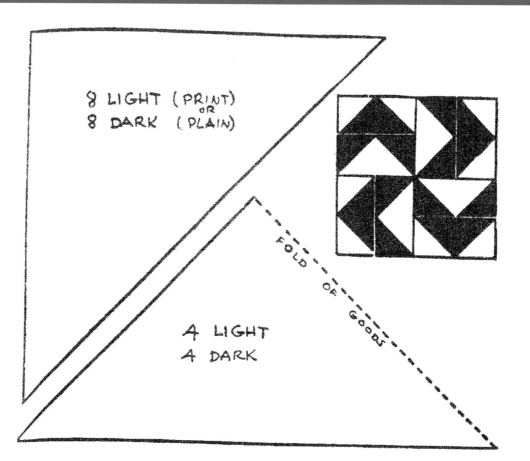

WINDING BLADES

8 LIGHT (PRINT) OR 8 DARK (PLAIN)

FOLD OF GOODS

4 LIGHT 4 DARK

Published August 4, 1943

The original instructions: **This is the pattern used by Mrs. E.L. Gravitt, Route 1, Tahlequah, Ok., when she pieced her first quilt, seventeen years ago. She says it is very easily cut and put together.**

IN *THE STAR*...

The idea behind the Agricultural Adjustment Act of the early 1930s was to help increase farm income by regulating production — and thus prices — of certain crops. By the time this pattern was published, in the middle of World War II, the plan was shunted aside for one allowing farmers more freedom in planting.

Star.

PRICE:

Minor Role For the AAA In Wartime Food Direction

"Crop Control" Program Is Out While the New WFA Plans to Guide Production With Price Inducements, but Leaving Farmer Free in His Choice of Crops.

The following article was written by Ovid A. Martin, Associated Press correspondent who covers the Department of Agriculture in Washington. Mr. Martin at one time headed the Associated Press bureau in Topeka and worked also in Missouri.

ment decide that more dry beans and fewer sugar beets were needed, it would provide prices which would make beans a better paying proposition than beets in areas where the two crops are interchangeable.

Shifts in other crops would be handled in similar manner.

Price Incentives to Production.
The government will use price

■ **Block size:** 12 inches
■ **Fabrics needed:** Two fabrics, a **light** and a **dark**.

CUTTING AND PIECING INSTRUCTIONS

NOTE: The following cutting measurements include a ¼-inch seam allowance.

■ From the **light** fabric, cut:
  * Eight 3⅞-inch squares.

■ From the **dark** fabric, cut:
  * Eight 3⅞-inch squares.

■ **Draw** a diagonal line from corner to corner on the wrong side of the light 3⅞-inch squares. Place each light 3⅞-inch square atop a dark 3⅞-inch square, right sides facing.

■ **Sew** ¼ inch on both sides of the diagonal line. Cut on the line and press toward the dark fabric.

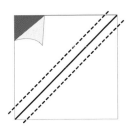

You will have 16 units that look like this:

■ **Assemble** the units in rows as shown.

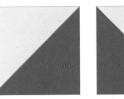

■ Make four of these units.

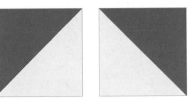

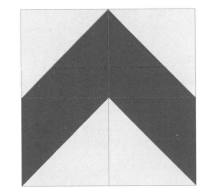

■ Assemble the four units as shown.

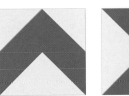

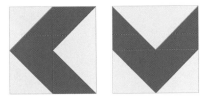

■ The finished block should look like this:

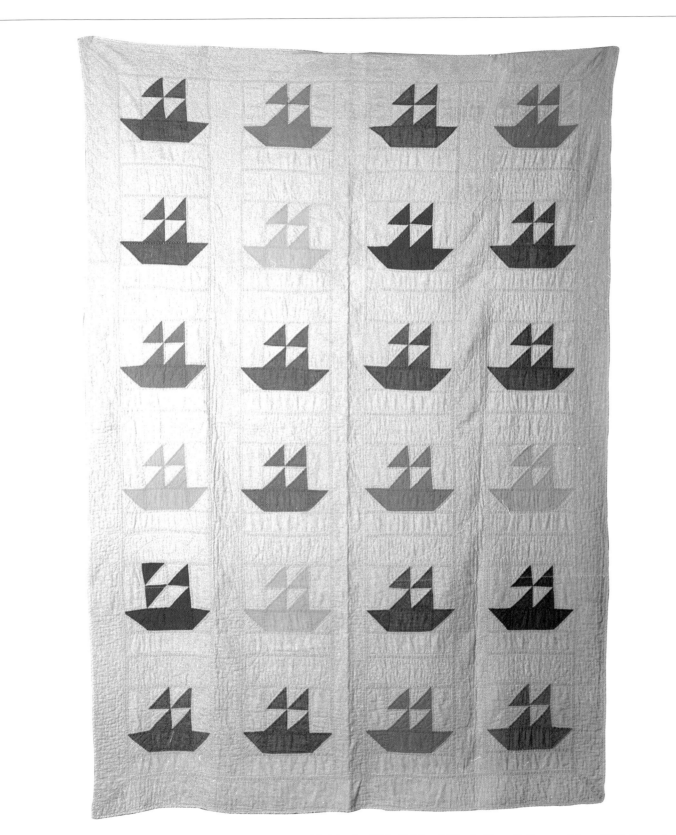

This quilt, called the Sail Boat by its owner, was made in 1940 by Sue Wakefield and Mattie Carroll. It resembles a 1936 *Star* pattern called Mayflower, but reverses the sails. In *The Star*'s 1945 Sail Boat in Blue and White, the sails also face the opposite direction as this quilt, and a blue strip is added to represent water. This quilt is owned by Nancy P. Wakefield of Platte City, Mo.

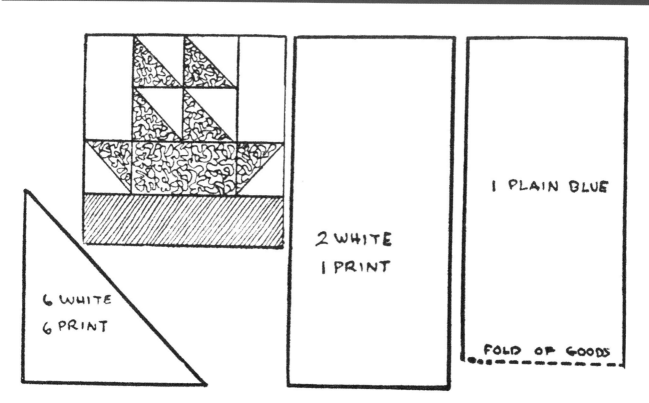

A SAIL BOAT IN BLUE AND WHITE

6 WHITE
6 PRINT

2 WHITE
1 PRINT

1 PLAIN BLUE

FOLD OF GOODS

Published Nov. 21, 1945

The original instructions: **The Sail Boat design is one which was created by Mrs. Eli Roberts, Plattsburg, Mo., for a baby bed. It is just as pretty, she says, for a large bed.**

IN *THE STAR...*

In 1945, the United States celebrated its first peacetime Thanksgiving in four years and the weekly *Star* marked the eve of the occasion with a big article and photographs on Missouri turkey farms. The Long-Miller operation in Clay County was begun on a small scale a decade earlier. It expanded rapidly, according to Leon Miller of the farm, when he realized that "under scientific management a turkey would make a pound of meat on less feed than any other farm animal." He also hinted at why turkeys' intelligence has been held in low esteem. His birds were contained in a fence less than a yard high, although they were capable of flying over it easily. "If the fence were six feet high," Miller told *The Star*, "we couldn't hold them. But this fence.... They just walk up to it, decide it isn't high enough to challenge their flying ability, and stay inside."

■ **Block size:** 12 inches
■ **Fabrics needed:** Three fabrics, a **light,** a **medium** and a **dark.**

CUTTING AND PIECING INSTRUCTIONS

NOTE: The following cutting measurements include a ¼-inch seam allowance.

■ From the **light** fabric, cut:
 * Three 3 ⅞-inch squares.
 * Two 3 ½-inch strips, each 6 ½ inches long.

■ From the **medium** fabric, cut:
 * One 3 ½-inch strip, 12 ½ inches long.

■ From the **dark** fabric, cut:
 * Three 3 ⅞-inch squares.
 * One 3 ½-inch strip, 6 ½ inches long.

■ **Draw** a diagonal line from corner to corner on the wrong side of the light 3 ⅞-inch squares. Place each light 3 ⅞-inch square atop each dark 3 ⅞-inch square, right sides facing.

■ **Sew** ¼ inch on both sides of the diagonal line. Cut on the line.

■ **Unfold** and press toward the dark fabric. You will have six half-square units that look like this:

■ **Sew** four half-square units together as shown.

■ **Sew** the dark strip to the half-square units.

■ **Sew** the remaining two half-square units to each light 6 ½-inch strip as shown.

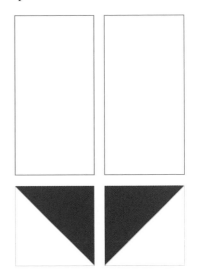

■ **Assemble** the units and the remaining medium strip as shown.

Sailboat block

Made by Edie McGinnis

A Scrap Zigzag block

Made by Edie McGinnis

Memory Bouquet (1930 pattern)

Made by Charlene Dodson.
Owned by Dorothymae Groves of Kansas City, Mo.

THE MEMORY BOUQUET QUILT

returns to The Star in its completed form

In autumn 1930, *The Kansas City Star* published a series of 20 applique blocks and a border design for a quilt called Memory Bouquet. The quilt designs were drawn by Eveline Foland, whose patterns were known for their art-deco style and her distinctive signature. After an introductory paragraph, each applique pattern was accompanied by the same directions, repeated with each pattern. Here are the directions as published in *The Star* beginning Oct. 13, 1930. On the pages after this, the introductory paragraph unique to each pattern appears, but the directions are not repeated.

The original instructions, as published each week:

The designs should be appliqued on fine white muslin or broadcloth. Cut each block 9 x 12 inches. If the white fabric used as a background is fine enough it may be placed over paper and the pattern traced in the middle of the block in pencil. Otherwise use carbon paper for tracing.

First, trace this pattern in the center of the white block. Second, trace the floral design on the different colored materials, allowing for seams for each petal, leaf and stem. Third, turn narrow hems and applique, following traced pattern on white block. Bowls may be appliqued in any color desired. The narrow stems may be embroidered in six-strand embroidery thread. Applique the heavier ones. Join completed blocks by 4-inch strips of green material

N.B. — These designs may be done in colored embroidery threads, using outline stitch. Designs also may be used for pillows, cushions, lamp shades, waste paper baskets, corners of curtains, bedspreads and paneled on doors of children's cupboards.

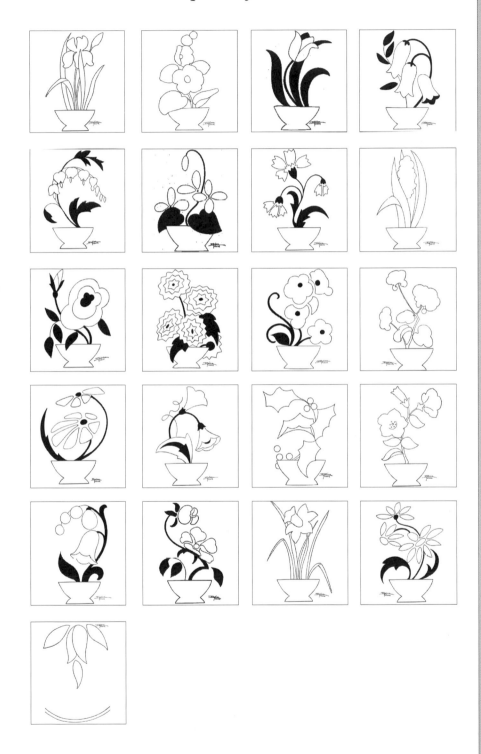

Published Oct. 13, 1930

This is the first of a series of twenty floral appliques. The leaves may be done in two shades of green, the standing petals of the flower a light lavender and the bud and the falling leaves of the flower purple. The bowl may be light green or any other desired color. The leaf overlapping the flower should be appliqued before the flower is done.

HOLLYHOCK

Published Oct. 14, 1930

Second in the series of twenty floral motifs comes the gay hollyhock. The bottom flower would be pretty done in deep rose with a cream center, the center flower light pink with the petal folded over deep rose, the next bud deep rose and the top one light pink. The bottom leaves are dark green, the back side of the leaf showing a lighter green, the two top leaves a light green. The same light green tone is used for the bowl and the strips that join the blocks.

Published Oct. 15, 1930

The tulip, a familiar motif to quilt fans, is the third in the series.

The applique of the brilliant tulip may be in a variety of colors, either red, yellow, or pink, with the leaves green and the bowl any desired color.

CANTERBURY BELL

Published Oct. 17, 1930

Fourth in the series is an especially lovely block, the old-fashioned Canterbury bell. The three bells are of light lavender — the bottom one having a facing of brilliant pink. The leaves are in two tones of green, the stems dark green and the thin stems embroidered with 6-strand thread. The bowl is in light green.

Eveline
Foland

Published Oct. 18, 1930

The delicate rose pink of the bleeding heart applique pattern, fifth in the series, in the floral quilt will carry the memory back to the old-fashioned garden.

Published Oct. 20, 1930

The appliqued pattern of the violet needs no direction as to color, a violet is a violet the world over. Two tones of lavender or yellow will be appropriate. The dots in the center of the flowers should be embroidered in black. Care should be taken to make the stem as narrow as possible. The leaves should be dark green, also the stem. The violet is the sixth in a series of twenty floral blocks.

Eveline Foland

Published Oct. 21, 1930

The appliqued pattern of the carnation, seventh in the series, will carry a bright motif in the garden quilt. Its slender leaves are dark green.

HYACINTH

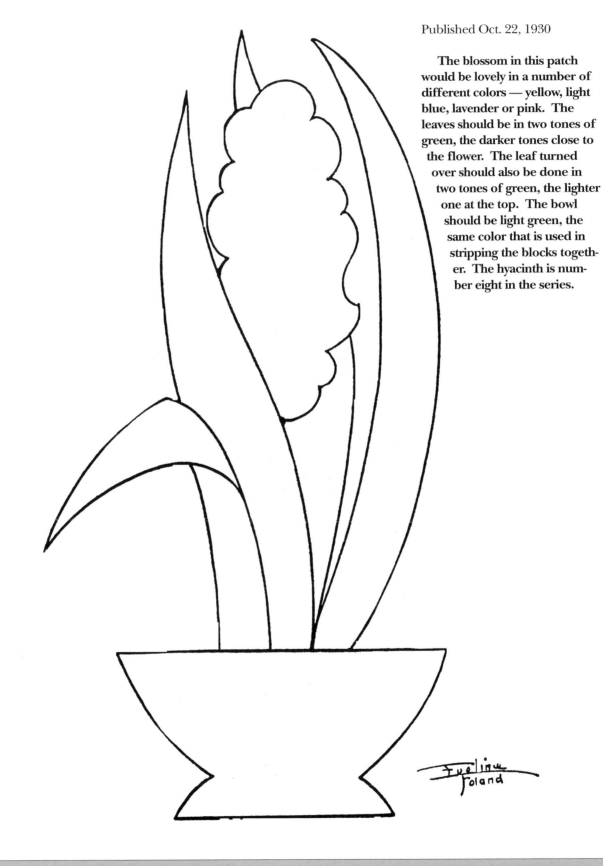

Published Oct. 22, 1930

The blossom in this patch would be lovely in a number of different colors — yellow, light blue, lavender or pink. The leaves should be in two tones of green, the darker tones close to the flower. The leaf turned over should also be done in two tones of green, the lighter one at the top. The bowl should be light green, the same color that is used in stripping the blocks together. The hyacinth is number eight in the series.

DOUBLE ROSE

Published Oct. 23, 1930

    The rose should be done in three shades of pink; deep rose for the center, very light pink next and pink on the outside. The bud should be done in the two darker shades, and the leaves in two shades of green, the stems in the darker tone. The very narrow stem should be embroidered in 6-strand floss the same shade as the other stems. This is the ninth pattern in the series of twenty.

Published Oct. 24, 1930

Half through the series! Today's is the tenth pattern in the complete series of twenty. The applique pattern of the ragged zinnia may be made in any color in which the flower blooms, delicate pinks, brilliant reds, or shades of orange. This conventionalized pattern is a series of applique in color. The leaves are in green.

Published Oct. 25, 1930

The appliqued pattern of the primrose, eleventh in the series, may be made in the color of that flower, which is pink with purplish cast. The leaves are in dark green shade.

GERANIUM

Published Oct. 27, 1930

If you are planning your memory bouquet quilt in soft colors, of course, the red geranium will be out of harmony, but there is a lovely salmon which will fit beautifully and look particularly pretty with the two tones of green used in the leaves. The stems should be of the deeper green, also the under part of the leaf whose edge is turned. The narrowest part of the stem should be done with 6-strand embroidery floss. The geranium is twelfth in the series.

Published Oct. 28, 1930

The colors of the black-eyed Susan, thirteenth in the series, are yellow and brown. The daisylike petals are appliqued in rich yellow and the centers in brown. The green foliage of the leaves adds a nice note of contrast.

Published Oct. 29, 1930

The freshness of the morning glory can be reproduced by making the full-blown flower in a deep rose or orchid, pale blue or pink. The stems and the leaves that curl about the base of the flower are developed in dark green. The leaves should be done in two tones of green — the darker being appliqued on the lighter, after it is sewed on. The stems should be dark green, the very narrow one embroidered in the same shade of the green as the other stems with 6-strand embroidery floss. This is the fourteenth of the series.

HOLLY

Published Oct. 31, 1930

The holly berries will be red, of course. The center leaf with the edge turned back should be in two tones of green, the darker used for the part turned over. The other three leaves should be dark green. The top stem, which is very narrow, should be embroidered in the same shade of green as the leaves, the wider stems at the bottom, dark green. This is the fifteenth in the series of twenty.

Published Nov. 1, 1930

The petunia can be done in a number of colors — pink, lavender and rose. The leaves should be done in two tones of green; the darker one being used for the stem. The stamens and the line showing the throat of both flowers should be embroidered in the same color as the flower. The bowl should be light green. This is number sixteen in the series.

Eveline Toland

Published Nov. 3, 1930

The dainty bell-like applique of the lily of the valley, seventeenth in the series, would be attractive appliqued in either yellow or orchid. The full-blown lily should be developed in the brightest shade and the buds gradations of the same colors. The long slender leaves will be in a clear dark green.

Published Nov. 4, 1930

The faint blush of the wild rose can be reproduced in the Memory Bouquet quilt by choosing a rose pink for the petals of the full blown flower and a slightly lighter tone for the bud. The two tones of green may be used for the stem, the lighter tone being used next to the flower. The leaves are in the darker tone. This is eighteenth in the series of twenty.

Published Nov. 5, 1930

The yellow jonquil will be a colorful reminder of a garden in full blossom. The long spear-like leaves may be developed in a dark tone of green with the bowl in a lighter tone of the same color if desired. This is nineteenth in the series.

Published Nov. 6, 1930

The variegated colors of the cosmos offer a wide selection for the cosmos applique. Any of the pink or lavender tones will be pretty with the center of the flower in yellow or brown. The leaves are dark green. This is the twentieth and the last of the flowers. Tomorrow's applique will be the border design.

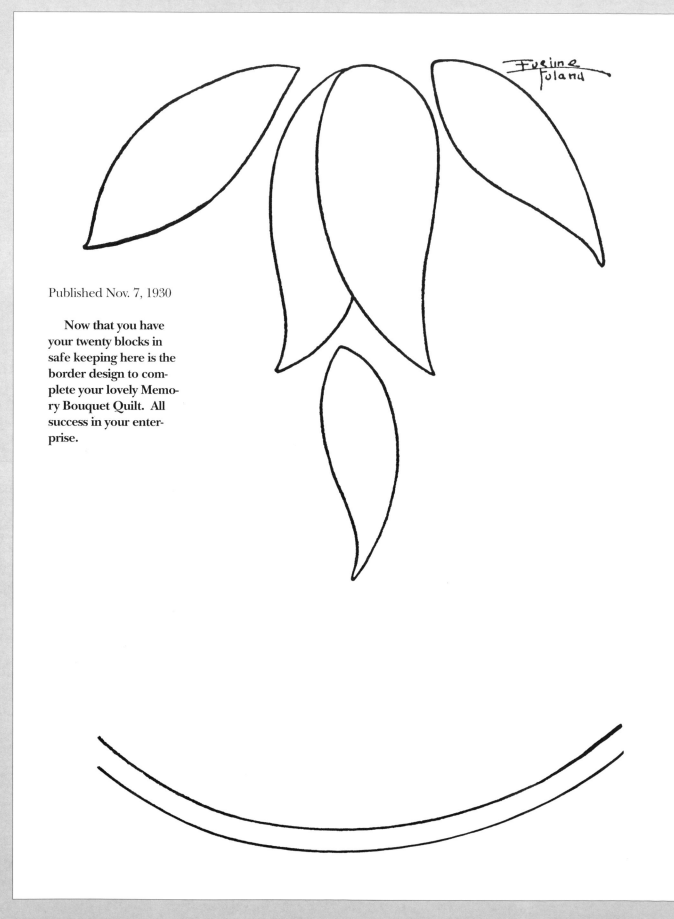

Published Nov. 7, 1930

Now that you have your twenty blocks in safe keeping here is the border design to complete your lovely Memory Bouquet Quilt. All success in your enterprise.

QUILTING DESIGNS

Sometimes *The Kansas City Star* ran quilting designs, used in stitching through the top, middle and bottoms layers of a quilt. Typically, these designs were applied to empty squares that quilters placed among blocks.

The decorative effect of quilted designs was obvious. It was one more way for old-time quilters to bring a touch of beauty into difficult and lonely lives on the farms and ranches of prairies and plain.

But quilting designs also had a practical effect. In the old days, quilt batting often was made at home, carded from cotton or wool. This batting could shift or shred unless it was tightly stitched into small compartments. Hand-stitchers took pride in how many stitches they could make in a small area; good stitchers could get 20 to the inch.

Even with today's modern, manufactured batting — unlikely to shred or shift — it's considered bad form to leave unstitched any area larger than four inches. The top, batting and backing can separate from one another, leading to a messy look and possibly wrinkles. These quilting designs are an attractive way to prevent that problem.

Some examples of the use of quilting designs. Top and above left by Edie McGinnis, above right by Sue Spade. These are not among the designs shown in the following pages.

Published Dec. 29, 1937

This circular design will fit almost any quilt block. If too small, add circular wavy lines to the outside; if too large, omit outside lines.

FOLD HERE

FOLD HERE

THE DOGWOOD QUILTING PATTERN

Published Sept. 5, 1934

 This is one-fourth of the dogwood, a flower familiar to Missourians. Trace this pattern in four sections and you have the entire pattern. If you desire closer lines of quilting add a line of quilting inside the petals of the flower.

FOLD HERE

FOLD HERE

Published Oct. 27, 1937

The many quilts made by the fans demand artistic designs for quilting. This one is one-fourth of the whole design, which may be made to one by folding the cloth to be quilted. Good luck to all of you.

A CONVENTIONAL PATTERN FOR QUILTING

Published Nov. 10, 1937

This modified floral pattern is one-fourth of the full size which is indicated by the fold along two sides of the pattern. Trace and quilt on any desired quilt or cushion.

Published Nov. 21, 1934

Now that the greatest clothes designers of the world have recognized the beauty and the decorative value of quilting on coats, blouses, collars and muffs, the circular motif lends itself to these uses, as well as to the quilt block.

Published Dec. 22, 1937

This design of which one-fourth is given, can be easily traced. Unfolded it makes a choice design to be transferred to a quilt. Reduced it is fine for a pocket and in full size may be used for silk cushions which make lovely gifts. Quilting is now a decoration for cuffs and collars on blouses and dresses.

FOLD HERE

FOLD HERE

Published Nov. 3, 1937

Again the floral motif is conventionalized for a quilting pattern. This is one-fourth of the pattern. Fold as indicated and trace for full pattern.

Published Nov. 14, 1934

No need to tell the fashion-wise woman the many uses of quilting. This square may decorate an evening coat or a quilt.

Published Nov. 17, 1937

This circular design will fit almost any quilt block. If too small, add circular wavy lines on the outside; if too large, omit outside lines.

A QUILTING MOTIF OF MANY USES

Published Jan. 5, 1938

    This is one of the quilting motifs that may be used in many ways. One-fourth of it or the entire pattern may be on quilts, cushions, silk or cotton robes or quilted bed-jackets.

Published Jan. 12, 1938

The quilted motif may be used for chair seats, cushions, and as a border on many household articles. Today it is also used on clothing, bed-jacket or a robe. This is one-fourth of the pattern.

TULIP AS A MOTIF IN QUILTING DESIGN

FOLD HERE

FOLD HERE

Published Dec. 8, 1937

    This lovely design for quilting uses the tulip as a motif. This is one-fourth of the whole design.

STAR PATTERN VARIATIONS

As any quilter knows, quilts amount to a lot more than the sum of their blocks. Blocks can be used lots of different ways to create interesting and often surprising patterns for the eye.

Watch how arranging and combining some of the blocks that you've just read about can create attractive and unexpected looks. Also, altering some of the colors (nevertheless maintaining the relationships of light, medium, dark and so forth) can create effective schemes.

These designs are the work of Jean Donaldson Dodd.

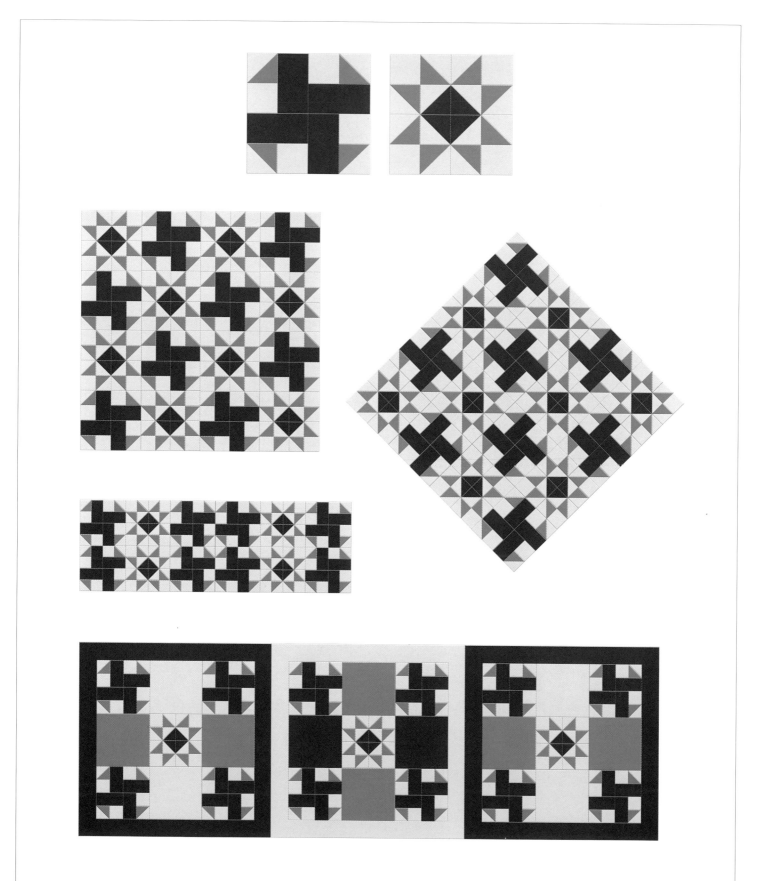

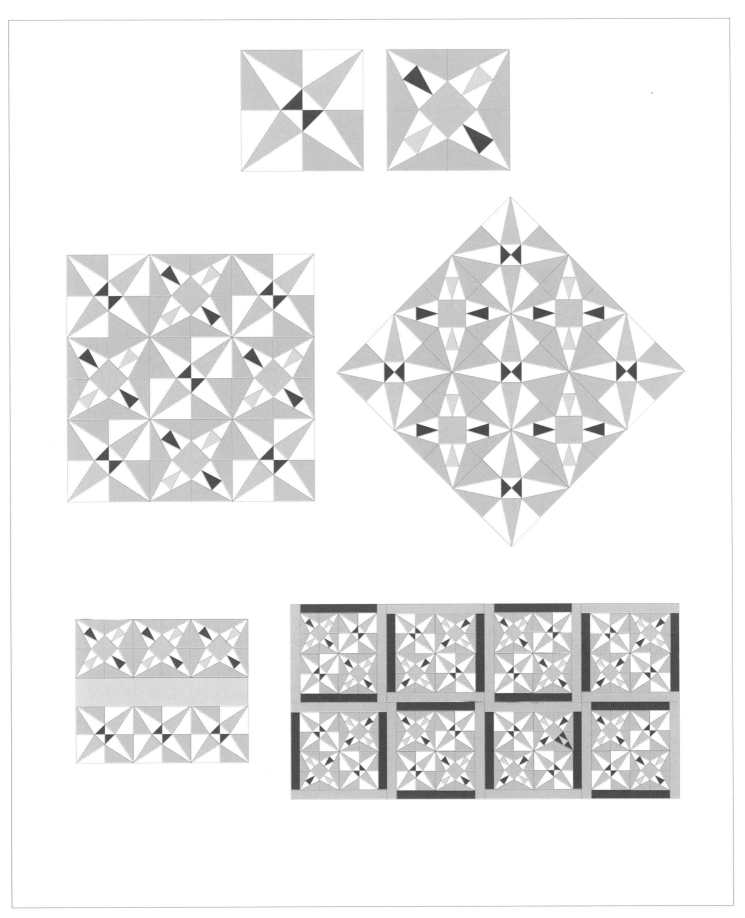

OTHER STAR QUILTS

Broken Star (1939 pattern)

Made in 1930's by Amanda Brazea.
Owned by Madelyn Goode of Kansas City, Mo.

Butterfly Quilt (1936 pattern)   **Owned by Dorothymae Groves of Kansas City, Mo.**

Circle Saw Quilt (1936 pattern)   **Made in 1987 by Marilyn Kneale Henderson of Kansas City, Mo.**

Crows Nest (1933 pattern)

Made by Ellen Groves in 1948.
Owned by Harold Groves of Kansas City, Mo.

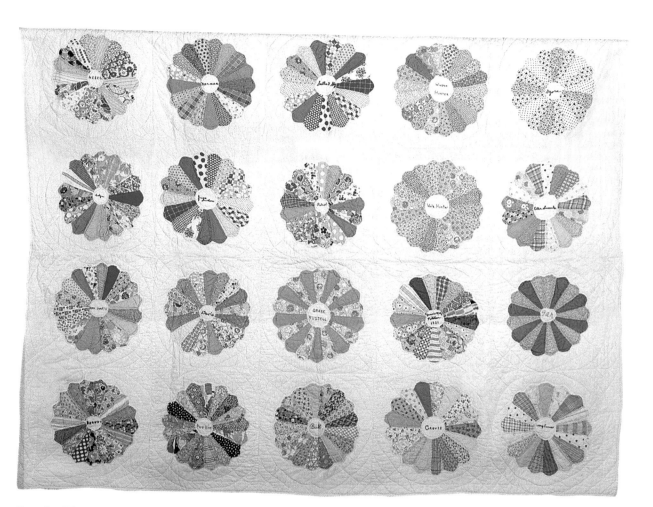

Dresden Plate Friendship Quilt (1931 pattern)

Made by Ethel Groves. Owned by Harold Groves

Old Fashioned Indian Puzzle (1959 pattern)   **Owned by Elizabeth S. Wallis of Overland Park, Kan.**

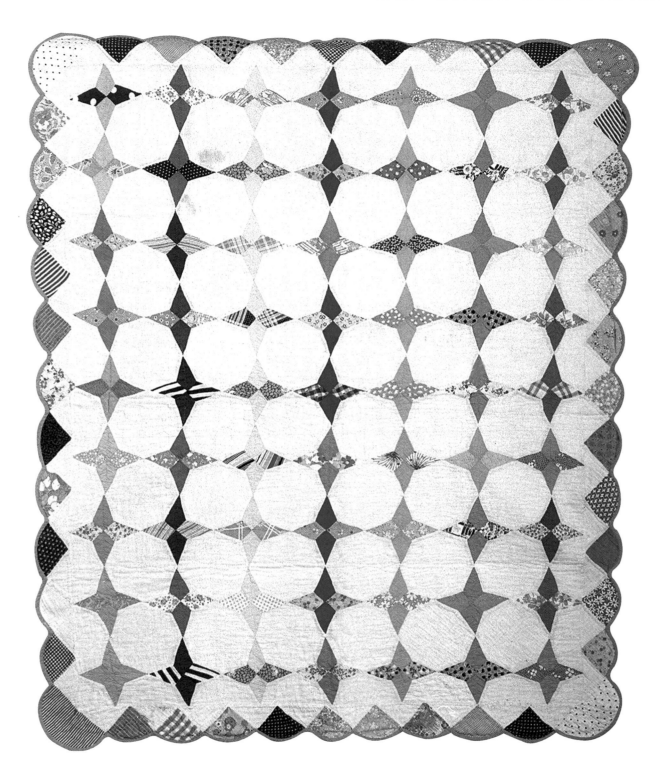

Kite Quilt (1931 pattern)   **Made by Ethel Groves. Owned by Harold Groves**

Log Cabin Quilt (1932 pattern)　　　　　　　　**Made in 1997 by Debby Hanlan of Stewartsville, Mo.**

Rose Dream Quilt (1930 pattern)

Made by Ethel Groves.
Owned by Harold Groves.

Square and 1/2 square (1933 pattern)

Made in 1939 by Alice Page.
Owned by Nancy Wakefield of Platte City, Mo.

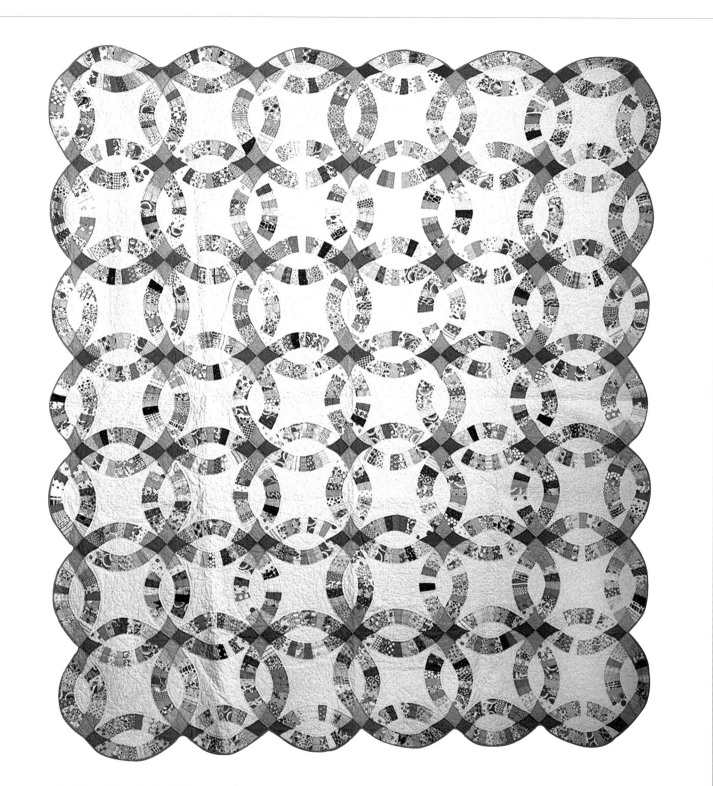

Wedding Ring Quilt (1928 pattern)

Made by Zola McCann
Owned by Shirley McCann of Overland Park, Kan.

Jacob's Ladder Quilt (1928 pattern)

Courtesy of Smiths Antiques, Laclede, Mo.

The Dutch Tile Quilt (1931 pattern)

Courtesy of Smiths Antiques, Laclede, Mo.

Lone Star Quilt (1930 pattern)   **Made in 1996 by Debby Hanlan of Stewartsville, Mo.**

With more than 1,000 patterns, the Kansas City Stars offer projects for everyone from novices to advanced quilters.

If you're a beginner but would like to try making an entire quilt, here are basic, complete directions for a full-size (72-by-96-inch) Double Square. Quilting books with more detailed instructions are available at quilt shops or your public library.

Terms in boldface are defined in the accompanying glossary.

Diagram 1

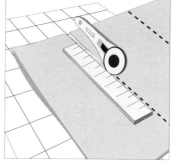

Diagram 2

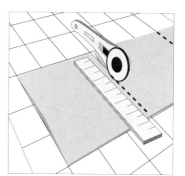

Diagram 3

Cutting

Machine-wash each fabric separately, using the detergent and temperature settings you plan to use to clean it after it becomes a quilt. Check for shrinkage and color fastness. With most modern fabrics, neither of these is a problem, but occasionally fabrics can shrink and colors can run. You don't want to find this out after your quilt is finished. If all is well, press each fabric and trim off **selvages** using your rotary cutter and rotary ruler.

Make sure all fabric edges are straight. Do this by folding the fabric in half lengthwise and aligning the long edges with horizontal lines on a rotary cutting mat. If edges along the width aren't straight, align your rotary-cutting ruler with a vertical line and cut straight across the width as close to the edge as possible to save fabric (Diagram 1).

Materials

These are available at quilt or craft stores.
Words in **boldface** are defined in the glossary at the end of this chapter.

4½ yards of dark fabric, 100 percent cotton
3½ yards of light fabric, 100 percent cotton
7½ yards of fabric for **backing**, 100 percent cotton
Double/queen size **batting** (cotton or polyfill)
Template plastic with grids
Rotary cutter

Rotary mat
Pins
Quilting thread
Quilting needles (betweens)
Quilting thimble
Wash-out marking pencils
24-by-6-inch clear ruler with grids
Quilting hoop

Now move the ruler 6¾ inches in from the edge and cut across the width of the fabric (Diagram 2). Repeat until you have 16 strips of dark fabric and 16 of light. Set aside remaining dark material for later use. Line up strips and cut into 6¾-inch squares (Diagram 3).

Cut these squares from corner to corner at a 45-degree angle (Diagram 4). You will have 192 dark triangles and 192 light triangles.

Piecing

You can **piece** your quilt by hand or machine. There are advantages to each.

With hand piecing, you don't need a sewing machine. Your project is portable. You can hand-piece just about anywhere, and many quilters enjoy taking their projects along with them.

Machine piecing, however, is a lot faster.

For this quilt, if you're piecing by hand: Place your template over the template pattern for the Double Square (See page 143). Trace on dashed lines. Cut out template with scissors.

Place the template on the **wrong side** of the fabric. Trace around the template with marking pencil on each triangular piece of fabric. These are sewing lines.

If you're piecing by machine, marking your sewing lines isn't necessary. Use the ¼-inch **seam guide** on your machine.

With the **right sides** of the fabric facing each other, place together the long sides of 1 light triangle and 1 dark triangle. Match the corners along the long side and pin on the seam line. With a small **running stitch**, sew along the marked seam line. Unfold and you'll have a square that is half dark and half light (Diagram 5).

Repeat on 3 more sets of triangles for a total of 4 squares.

Sew 2 squares together, placing dark triangle against light as shown in Diagram 6. Sew 2 more squares together the same way.

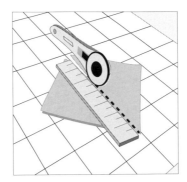

Diagram 4

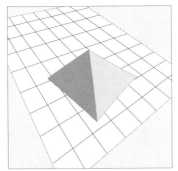

Diagram 5

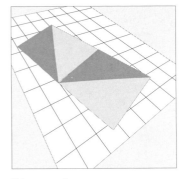

Diagram 6

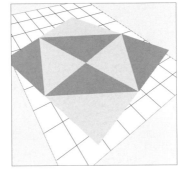

Diagram 7

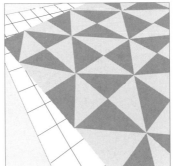

Diagram 8

Diagram 9

Place those 2 rectangles together and sew as shown in Diagram 7. This makes 1 complete block.

Repeat the process until 48 blocks are complete.

Sew 6 blocks together into strip. Make 8 strips. Sew strips together to complete the **quilt top** (Diagram 8). Before you sew together each block and each strip, pin each part together, taking care to keep all corners and intersecting seams matched.

Backing

Fold the backing fabric in half lengthwise. Cut across the width into two parts, each 3¾ yards long. Place the parts together, right sides facing each other. Sew pieces together along the length of fabric.

This forms the back of the quilt.

Assembly

Iron the quilt top with all **seams** going toward the dark piece. On the back, press the middle seam open. This makes it easier to quilt through the seam.

Place backing, right side *down*, on a flat surface; smooth out all wrinkles. Place the quilt **batting** atop the backing. Place the top on these, right side *up*. **Baste** all layers together with thread or safety pins 4 to 6 inches apart in a rough grid. If you baste with thread, remove the stitches only after finishing the quilting. If you use safety pins, remove them as you quilt.

Quilting

You are now ready to begin **quilting**.

Place your quilting hoop as near the center as possible. You'll work from the center out toward the edges, moving the hoop as you complete each area.

Thread your quilting needle and put a small knot at one end of the thread. Thread directly from the spool to minimize tangles.

Mark the quilting line on each block ¼ inch in from each seam line with fine-line, wash-out marking pencil or with ¼-inch quilter's masking tape.

To start the first stitch, slide the needle in anywhere under the first layer and pull the needle up to a marked quilting line. Tug gently until the knot pulls through the starting point and catches between the layers. That way, the knot will be hidden

Continue quilting as shown in Diagram 9. Try to make stitches as small and even as possible.

When you're almost out of thread, tie a knot in the thread closest to the quilt top. Insert your needle through the top layer, through the batting and back out the top, lodging the knot in the batting. Cut the remaining thread, rethread the needle and repeat the process.

Binding

After all quilting is complete, you'll need to **bind** the quilt.

Trim all excess batting and backing from the edges. Using the dark fabric set aside earlier, cut 10 strips horizontally, each 2½ inches wide.

Sew the ends of 2 strips together across their width. The resulting strip will be long enough to go across the top edge of the quilt. Sew 2 more strips together in the same

Diagram 10

Diagram 11

Diagram 12

manner to go across the bottom edge of the quilt. Now sew 3 strips together to go on each side of the quilt. Fold each strip in half lengthwise and press (Diagram 10). Then fold one side of each strip halfway in and press. Bring the other side over until edges meet and press again (Diagram 11).

Sew the strip to the top of quilt with a running stitch (Diagram 12). Turn the remaining binding to the back and stitch. Do the side edges of the quilt first. Then do the top and bottom edges, folding under the raw ends of the binding to make the corners neat.

Your *Kansas City Star* quilt is complete!

QUILT GLOSSARY

■ **Background (or secondary) fabric:** A secondary fabric that complements the predominant fabric used in a quilt. (See also *primary fabric.*)

■ **Backing:** The bottom layer of a quilt.

■ **Baste:** Pinning or loosely stitching layers of a quilt together in preparation for quilting. The pins or stitches are later removed and the quilting holds all the layers of the quilt together.

■ **Batting:** The middle layer of the quilt, which provides depth and warmth. Batting, mainly cotton or polyester, is sold in lofts; a high loft is thick, a low loft is thin. The thinner the loft, the easier it is to quilt.

■ **Binding:** A strip of fabric used to enclose the rough edges of all the layers of a finished quilt.

■ **Block:** A square unit consisting of pieces of fabric sewn into a design. Many blocks sewn together make a quilt top.

■ **4-patch:** A square block using four pieces of fabric.

■ **9-patch:** A square block using nine pieces of fabric.

■ **Piecing:** Stitching together quilt pieces.

■ **Press to, press away:** To iron the fabric in a block. "Press to dark" means iron both sides of the seam toward the darker fabric; "press to the edge" means iron both sides of the seam toward the outer edge of the fabric, and so on. "Press away" means the opposite, as in "press away from center."

■ **Primary fabric:** The predominant fabric used in a quilt.

■ **Quilting:** Stitching through the top, middle and bottom layers of a quilt in a design or in straight lines to secure the layers together and add a decorative touch.

■ **Quilting hoop:** A two-part wooden or plastic circle. Placed on either side of the quilt, the hoop holds the fabric taut inside.

■ **Quilting needles:** Smaller than sewing needles, quilting needles are called "betweens." They come in sizes from 7 (longest) to 12 (shortest). Beginning quilters often use a 7 or 8.

■ **Quilting thimble:** A thimble with a ridge around the top to help push the quilting needle.

■ **Quilting thread:** Heavier and stronger than average sewing thread.

■ **Right side:** The front side of the fabric with a pattern or color; the opposite of the "wrong side," or back of a fabric.

■ **Rotary cutter:** A sharp, circular cutting utensil — resembling a pizza cutter — used to cut through layers of fabric.

■ **Rotary mat:** A mat marked with grids and angles, made to be used with a rotary cutter.

■ **Running stitch:** A sewing stitch made by passing the needle in and out repeatedly, using short, even stitches.

■ **Selvages:** The lengthwise, finished edges of a fabric.

■ **Seams:** The line formed by sewing together pieces of fabric.

■ **Seam guide:** A mark or piece on a sewing machine footplate that measures the distance from the needle to the edge of the fabric.

■ **Template:** A pattern, usually plastic, used to trace cutting or sewing lines onto fabric.

■ **Wrong side:** See **Right side.**

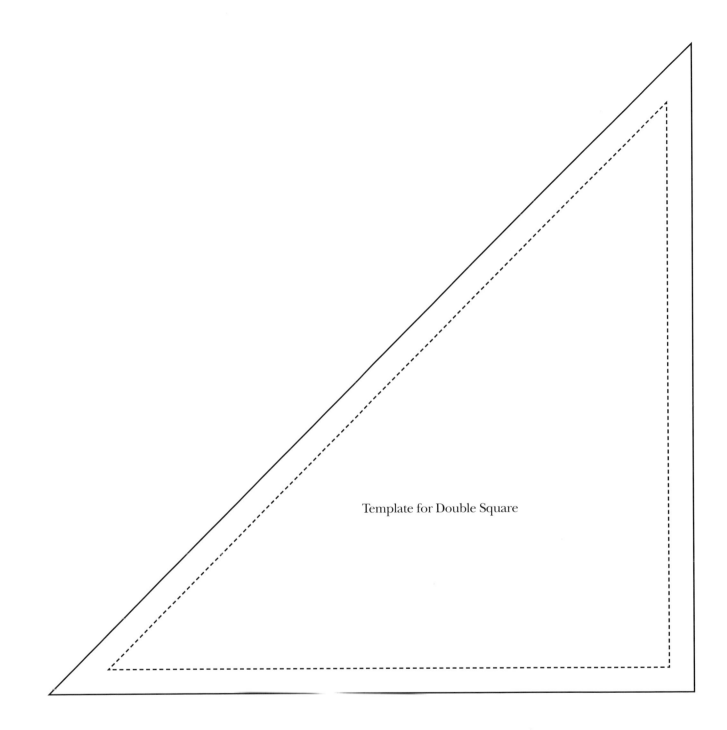

Template for Double Square

Here is a chronological list — including repeats — of the quilt patterns and designs published by *The Kansas City Star* from 1928 through 1961.

If you'd like to see the patterns on the pages of the newspaper, microfilm copies of *The Star* are available at the Kansas City Public Library's Main Branch, 311 E. 12th St., Kansas City, Mo.

For an alphabetical list of the designs, see Wilene Smith's

Quilt Patterns: An Index to The Kansas City Star Patterns (details in Bibliography).

For a thumbnail sketch of each pattern, see Volume 5 of *The Ultimate Illustrated Index to The Kansas City Star Quilt Pattern Collection* by the Central Oklahoma Quilters Guild (details in Bibliography).

Months not listed here had no published quilt patterns.

1928

■ **September**
Pine Tree
Album Quilt
■ **October**
French Star
Log Cabin
Rob Peter and Pay Paul
Cherry Basket
Wedding Ring
■ **November**
Jacob's Ladder
Greek Cross
Sky Rocket
Double T
■ **December**
Ocean Wave
Wild Goose Chase
Old Maid's Puzzle
Rambler

1929

■ **January**
Weathervane
Monkey Wrench
Spider Web
Irish Chain
■ **February**
Rising Sun
Princess Feather
Double Nine Patch
Eight-Pointed Star
■ **March**
Goose in the Pond
Dove in the Window
Beautiful Star
Broken Circle
Beggar Block
■ **April**
Cupid's Arrow Point
Noon Day Lily
Lafayette Orange Peel
Necktie
■ **May**
Duck and Ducklings
House on the Hill
Crossed Canoes
Turkey Tracks
■ **June**
Ribbon Border Block
Posey

Bird's Nest
Crosses and Losses
Double Star
■ **July**
Jack in the Box
Aircraft
Springtime Blossoms
Sunbeam
■ **August**
Saw-Tooth
Cross and Crown
Hands All 'Round
Honey Bee
Flower Pot
■ **September**
Susannah
Goose Tracks
Fish Block
Wedding Ring
■ **October**
Swastika
Seth Thomas Rose
"V" Block
Little Beech Tree
■ **November**
Palm Leaf
Tulip Applique
Mill Wheel
Order No. 11
Old King Cole's Crown
■ **December**
Strawberry Block
Old King Cole
Little Wooden Soldier
Road to Oklahoma
(The "Santa's Parade
   Quilt" series ran
   in December 1929).

1930

■ **January**
Churn Dash
Corn and Beans
Rose Cross
Milky Way
■ **February**
True Lovers Buggy Wheel
Indiana Puzzle
Blazing Star
Aster
■ **March**
Sunflower
Grape Basket
Steps to the Altar

Kaleidoscope
Dutchman's Puzzle
■ **April**
English Flower Garden
Single Wedding Ring
Pin Wheels
Cross and Crown
■ **May**
Missouri Puzzle
Merry Go-Round
Lone Star
Missouri Star
Sail Boat
■ **June**
Virginia Star
Rail Fence
■ **July**
Mexican Star
Basket of Oranges
Rose Album
Clay's Choice
■ **August**
Maple Leaf
Sunbonnet Sue
Compass
Kaleidoscope
Rainbow Tile
■ **September**
Goblet
Calico Puzzle
Broken Dishes
Swallows in the Window
■ **October**
Secret Drawer
Spider Web
Marble Floor
Pinwheel
(The "Memory Bouquet
   Quilt" series ran
   in October 1930.)
■ **November**
Grandmother's Favorite
Indian Emblem
Friendship
Puss in the Corner
Sage-Bud
(The "Memory Bouquet
   Quilt" series ran
   in November 1930).
■ **December**
Turnabout "T"
Snow Crystals
Sweet Gum Leaf
Rose Dream

1931

■ **January**
Silver and Gold
Tennessee Star
Flower Pot
Greek Cross
Sheep Fold
■ **February**
Amethyst
Wheel of Mystery
Pontiac Star
Baby Bunting
■ **March**
Seven Stars
Rebecca's Fan
French Bouquet
Casement Window
■ **April**
Basket of Lilies
King's Crown
June Butterfly
Fence Row
■ **May**
Indian Trail
English Ivy
Jackson Star
Dutch Tulip
Love Ring
■ **June**
Ararat
Iris Leaf
Ozark Diamond
Kite Quilt
■ **July**
Cactus Flower
Arrowhead Star
Giddap
Sugar Loaf
■ **August**
Cross Roads
Bachelor's Puzzle
Morning Star
Pineapple Quilt
Dresden Plate
■ **September**
Stepping Stones
Tennessee Star
Chips and Whetstones
Boutonniere
■ **October**
Prickly Pear
Castle Wall

Butterfly
Pickle Dish
Dutch Tile
■ **November**
Cottage Tulips
Formosa Tea Leaf
Bridge
Evening Star
■ **December**
Poinsettia
Goldfish
Christmas Star
Crazy Daisy

1932

■ **January**
Friendship Knot
Circular Saw
Heart's Desire
Job's Tears
Necktie
(The "Horn of Plenty
   Quilt" series also ran
   in January 1932).
■ **February**
Autograph Quilt
Hour-Glass
Spring Beauty
Grandmother's Basket
(The "Horn of Plenty
   Quilt" series also ran
   in February 1932).
■ **March**
Grandmother's Favorite
Quilting Design
Shamrock
Magnolia Bud
■ **April**
Nose-Gay
Diamond Field
Red Cross
Solomon's Puzzle
"4-H" Club
■ **May**
Russian Sunflower
Storm at Sea
Crow's Nest
Garden Maze
■ **June**
Cowboy's Star
Ducklings
Lend and Borrow
Wheel of Fortune
■ **July**

INDEX OF PATTERNS

INDEX OF PATTERNS

INDEX OF PATTERNS

INDEX OF PATTERNS

ACKNOWLEDGEMENTS

We owe special thanks to Betty Haynie of Gladstone, Mo., for her expert help in testing these patterns. For their help in finding several quilts made from Star patterns, we are grateful to Ruby Smith of Laclede, Mo., and Sharon McMillan of Marquette Heights, Ill. Peggy Hutinett gave much helpful advice, particularly with the difficult Star and Box pattern.

PHOTO CREDITS

All photos of quilts and blocks by Tammy Ljungblad, staff photographer of *The Kansas City Star*.

Other credits:

ii. Original drawing by L.L. Broadfoot from his book *Pioneers of the Ozarks*, copyright 1944. Reproduced by permission of Caxton Press, Caldwell, Idaho.

vii. Photo of *The Kansas City Star* building from the files of the newspaper.

viii. Photo of Edie McGinnis by Steve Gonzales of *The Kansas City Star*. Other photos from the files of the newspaper.

BIBLIOGRAPHY

Wilene Smith, *Quilt Patterns: An Index to The Kansas City Star Patterns, 1928-1961*. Mennonite Press, 1985. For more information write: Wilene Smith, 815 W. 61st North, Wichita, KS, 67204; or e-mail WileneSmth@aol.com.

Central Oklahoma Quilters Guild Inc., *The Ultimate Illustrated Index to the Kansas City Star Quilt Pattern Collection*. 1990. For more information write: Central Oklahoma Quilters Guild, P.O. Box 23916, Oklahoma City, OK, 73123.

Harold and Dorothymae Groves, editors and compilers, *The Kansas City Star Classic Quilt Patterns: Motifs & Designs* . 11 volumes, Groves Publishing Co., 1988. For more information write: Groves Publishing Co., P.O. Box 33068, Kansas City, MO, 64114